Earthly Delights

Earthly Delights

Gardening by the Seasons the Easy Way

MARGOT ROCHESTER

TAYLOR TRADE PUBLISHING

Lanham • New York • Dallas • Boulder • Toronto • Oxford

Published by Taylor Trade Publishing
An imprint of The Rowman & Littlefield Publishing Group, Inc.
4501 Forbes Boulevard, Suite 200
Lanham, Maryland 20706

Distributed by National Book Network

Library of Congress Cataloging-in-Publication Data

Rochester, Margot, 1935-
  Earthly delights : gardening by the seasons the easy way /
Margot Rochester.—1st Taylor Trade Pub. ed.
     p. cm.
  ISBN 1-58979-078-2 (hardcover : alk. paper)
  1. Gardening. I. Title.
SB453.R625 2004
635.9—dc22   2003023783

♾™ The paper used in this publication meets the minimum requirements of
American National Standard for Information Sciences—Permanence of Paper for
Printed Library Materials, ANSI/NISO Z39.48-1992.
Manufactured in the United States of America.

In memory of my mother,
Margot Peyser McAuliffe,
who should have had time to garden
1908–1954

CONTENTS

❧

Contents

PREFACE

꧁

This book began fifteen years ago when I sent a story about my coastal garden to the editor of the *Island Breeze,* a monthly newspaper on the Outer Banks of North Carolina. The column was accepted for publication and I was invited to continue writing for the *Breeze.* And was paid to do so!

Little did that editor know that the columns would have been written without pay. Little did I know that I was beginning an adventure that continues to this day and has become one of my life's most satisfying endeavors.

I have never lost the excitement of seeing my work in print or the feeling of surprise when strangers respond to something I write. Publication is an exhilarating and affirming experience.

Writing these columns has connected me to my garden and to other people's gardens in an extraordinary way. I quickly realized that gardening is more than gardening. It is a process of discovery about the world and about ourselves.

On a less mystical note, a garden is, or should be, a source of inordinate joy for the gardener. When a garden becomes laborious instead of a labor of love, when joy is lost, the gardener must change herself or the garden or both.

Earthly Delights: Gardening by the Seasons the Easy Way is about the changes I have experienced over the years, both in myself and in the gardens I have tended. Because I cannot imagine life without a garden, I have spent these writing and gardening years looking for ways to garden leisurely and efficiently so that limited time and increasing age would not hinder me.

My garden is in the South because that is where I live. However, I do not regard it as a Southern garden or myself as a Southern gardener. The plants I grow are limited or enhanced by our climate, but the strategies I use and the pleasure my garden gives me have nothing to do with state lines or first frost dates.

Actually, I have two gardens. One is on a coastal island. Buffeted by wind, tides, and salt spray as well as drought, this garden keeps me humble. I might consider it a failure if I did not find something to enjoy every single time I see it.

The other garden, the one most of this book is about, wraps around the house where we have lived for forty years. The lawn and grapevines belong to my husband, but the garden is mine and it is a treasure. Few days go by when I do not stroll among the borders and beds, enjoying the changes and surprises that never cease.

In this book, I share strategies and observations as gardeners share seeds and cuttings. We offer favorite bits of our garden to friends, assuming that someday they will pass them onto others. I can think of few human activities that enable participants to connect in this remarkable way with one another and with posterity.

Regard this book as a collection of offshoots, not from my garden but from my gardening life. I hope you will be entertained and informed, but, more than anything, I hope you will discover the joy of creating your own glorious garden, the easy way.

ACKNOWLEDGMENTS

To all the friends who have encouraged me along the way to publication, my gratitude is beyond words. They know who they are and why I love them.

I owe special thanks to readers who have stopped me in the grocery store and the post office and have called or e-mailed to tell me they liked something I had written. Writers need to be assured that their work is read.

I was a reader of garden books before I became a gardener. While still in college, I stumbled across Ruth Stout's book *How to Have a Green Thumb without an Aching Back*. Later I discovered Allen Lacy, who led me to Henry Mitchell and Elizabeth Lawrence, writers who introduced me to the small and grand pleasures of the garden. They not only set the standard for writing about gardens but they also let me know, before I ever picked up a trowel, that gardening was more than growing flowers and vegetables.

Of course, I am especially grateful to my editor at Taylor Publishing, Michael Emmerich, who was willing to take a chance on this late bloomer, and to Sharon Thompson, who read the manuscript three times, corrected my spelling and inaccuracies, and urged me onward.

Most of all, I am thankful to and for my husband, Dick, who, after forty-seven years, has almost adapted to my eccentricities and continually encourages me to flap my wings and see what happens. He and our sons, Tom and Dan; their wives, Cindy and Bonnie; and our grandchildren, Haley, Drew, Gray, Morgan, and Margot, will always be the greatest delights of my life.

CHAPTER 1

Breaking Ground

When a garden becomes laborious instead of a labor of love,
when joy is lost, the gardener must change herself
or the garden or both.

True Confessions of a Leisurely Gardener

You might as well learn the truth right off the bat. I am as lazy a gardener as you are likely to meet, even though I tend a mixed border of perennials, annuals, herbs, and shrubs that is about 100 feet long and over eight feet deep. In addition, I have a woodland garden as well as assorted beds I create or enlarge whenever the mood strikes and my husband is not paying attention.

I begin most days with a purposeful walk around my garden, sometimes for five minutes and sometimes, when one thing leads to another, for an hour or so. I always carry a pocketknife or clippers, because, if I had to stop my stroll and search for a tool when I am ready to snip a cutting or trim a wayward branch, I would forget my mission and start doing something else. On a purposeful walk, focus is everything.

Not only do I spend minimal time doing whatever tasks beckon on a particular day, but I am also away from my garden for weeks at a time even during the hottest part of the summer. Until a few years ago, I had no irrigation system other than that provided by Mother Nature, and we all know just how unreliable she is in July and August.

Let me tell you what else I do not do. I might as well reveal the whole truth at once. I do not till; I do not have a compost pile that needs turning; and I do not use herbicides, fungicides, or insecticides (except against fire ants, which I might nuke if I had the resources). I have a gardening staff of one, and she is writing this book.

The secret to my success and sunny disposition? My garden plots were originally lawn I left in place but blanketed with layers of newspaper, which, in turn, were covered with a thick layer of compost and then a layer of mulch. I continue to add shredded leaves, pinestraw, and hay for year-round mulch. In my coastal garden, I use dried seaweed. The goal is to find free or inexpensive mulching material and use it lavishly.

Contrary to expert advice, I never remove this mulch but let it incorporate itself into the soil, adding humus and tilth, which is the stuff those of us who garden in either clay or sand need badly. It is not long before earthworms come to the feast.

After all, is this not the natural process? In the woods, leaves drop and no one rakes. The only digging that occurs is that of entrepreneurs scraping soil from the woods to bag and sell. This is the stuff we buy! As a result of my on-the-spot mulching process, my sand has become sandy loam, dark and humusy, a pleasure to plant in and to show off to fellow gardeners.

When should you start mulching? Immediately, and never stop. When you finish reading the morning newspaper, add it to the pile you intended to take to the recycling center and start recycling in your own garden. Wherever weeds or unwanted grass grow, put down a newspaper layer eight to ten sheets thick, cover with the mulch of your choice, and, if no rain is imminent, hose down to settle the stack.

Make sure the newspaper sheets overlap so no light reaches the soil. The purpose of the newspaper is to deprive seeds and weeds of the light they need to germinate and grow. If you use mulch alone, weeds will probably grow right through, saying as they emerge, "Thank you for the shade." It is the newspaper layer that tells weeds you are serious.

Not only do I use newspaper to retain moisture and discourage weeds, but I also use the same process to start new beds and add to old ones. I put newspaper down (again, eight to ten sheets thick) where I want the new garden plot, cover it with mulch, wait a season or two, and the soil is ready to plant.

The newspaper decomposes slowly, weeds and grass are starved for light, and they give up the ghost. The soil is friable and moist, ready for planting, and I have not picked up a trowel, let alone a tiller.

Kitchen scraps (vegetable and fruit peels, leftovers that cannot be served one more time, scrapings from plates, eggshells, dryer lint—anything but meat or fat) go into a bucket under the sink. When the bucket is full I take it out to the garden, lift up some mulch, and tuck it in where it can do the most good.

I return the mulch I had removed, perhaps adding to it if it has thinned out, and stomp on the pile. The scraps quickly become compost and I have not gone through the laborious task of piling it up, brown on green, and turning it, let alone taking its temperature.

True Confessions of a Leisurely Gardener

So there you have it: the basic process that lets me be a leisurely gardener, liberating me from bothersome tasks such as weeding, tilling, digging up grass, or turning a compost pile. As a result, I am freed to pursue the far more pleasurable pastimes of picking, cutting, and feeling smug as I admire the view.

4

Just Say No to Unpleasant Tasks

My garden looks best as fall begins, but in early spring (or late winter, if you are a stickler for facts) every day brings surprises. It is my favorite time of the year. I love to discover new buds on deciduous shrubs, bright green leaves emerging from the earth, tiny seedlings breaking through the mulch. As I crawl around on hands and knees, I realize once again that I am a rich woman indeed.

Of course, many of these discoveries are true surprises because I continually forget where I put things . . . keys, glasses, pocketknives, larkspur . . . which gives me the opportunity to be overjoyed when I stumble across the missing items. I am a gardener with trowels and pruners scattered around the yard so I do not have to search too hard to find a tool before the urge to plant or trim evaporates.

At any rate, spring is a grand time to be a gardener. It is also a time when lots of gardening advice is bandied about, but it seems to me that much of this advice makes gardening sound unpleasant and problematic. All this talk about eradicating weeds and spraying roses and double-digging is enough to discourage anyone with a grain of laziness.

Why do we make growing seem difficult when it is a natural process that goes on quite well, thank you, without human assistance? Look at the forests, the marshes, the weed patch . . . happily thriving without our interference.

A garden is in many ways a struggle against nature. When we start a garden, the first task we have to do is clear out the natural vegetation and then mold the space to our liking: a hedge here, a perennial bed there, a tree placed just so.

That is the greatest joy of gardening, I think. We create Eden to our own taste. But we can also make our gardening lives easier and more fruitful if we think about what nature does quite well and about why we garden. If you garden because you enjoy arduous labor, self-destruction, and constant frustration, stop reading right now. We are from different planets.

I garden because I love watching plants grow, beginning with their emergence from the soil to their final adieu as crackling stalks and seedpods. I love the colors of every season and the joy of sharing with friends. I have neither time nor energy to waste on tasks that diminish my pleasure.

To my way of thinking, simple (and painless) gardening is preferable and kinder not only to me and my joints but to the environment as well. The following is a list of tasks I avoid:

1. I do not like the smell or feel of chemical fertilizers, so I do not use them and my garden flourishes.

2. I do not like to dig (and my husband is not crazy about it either), so I mulch where I want garden plots to be and let everything sit for a season or two until I have rich, friable, grassless earth for planting.

3. Until we installed a well, I did not water my garden more than three or four times between June and September, not because I disliked watering but because I was away much of the summer. I mulched my garden with three or four inches of pinestraw, hay, and shredded leaves. When I did water with soaker hoses hidden beneath the mulch, I saturated the soil to keep plant roots deep. Short spurts of watering encourage shallow roots that depend on the gardener to keep the moisture coming. I like plants (and people) to be self-reliant—or at least not to rely on me.

4. I do not like to weed and I certainly do not want to add herbicides to the water supply, so I mulch my garden with three or four inches of pinestraw, hay, and shredded leaves. (I know I have already said this, but mulch is worth repetition.) The few weeds that come up through the mulch are easily pulled from soft, moist earth. If weeds persist, I smother them with newspaper and more mulch. I am smarter, bigger, and more stubborn than any weed that shows up on my turf.

5. I do like to mow, but not a lot. Grass seems overrated to me as a visual delight, so I enlarge my borders and naturalized areas to cut down on turf. You may be thinking grass is pretty easy to care for compared to a perennial bed or vegetable patch, but which is worth doing well?

6. I hate, really hate, turning a compost pile and there is no chance my husband will volunteer to do it. Instead, I collect vegetable scraps, dryer lint, and other such stuff in a bucket under my kitchen sink. When my bucket is full, I take it to the garden and slip the contents under the mulch wherever I want some compost, stepping on it to break down the raw materials.

No matter how fierce winter has been, spring is bound to come, so get ready to enjoy your garden. Choose your objectives, set priorities, and concentrate your labor where it really matters. Garden to feast your eyes and stomach, to stir your soul, but certainly not to strain your back.

Give Me Five . . . or Ten

People who know my reluctant approach to housework will be surprised to know that I read the newspaper column, "Hints from Heloise." While I never cease to be amazed that there are rational human beings cleaning windowsills with Q-tips, I always appreciate suggestions for organizing my life.

A few weeks ago, Heloise gave this advice: "Think five." When you open a messy drawer, throw out five items. When you tidy your closet, get rid of five tired garments or empty shoe boxes. When you clean your desk, throw away five pieces of paper. Anyone can do this. Five is so doable, even for sluggards.

I wish I could tell you that this Rule of Five has changed my housekeeping habits and my home is now pristine. I cannot tell a lie, but I have eliminated a lot of stuff by forcing myself to discard at least five items at a time.

Not surprisingly, the Rule of Five has gone outdoors with me and now applies to weeds, brambles, pruning, plant moving, and other garden tasks. I see one briar, I pull it up and find at least four more before I stop. If I prune one wayward branch, I look around for four more before going on to more appealing pastimes. Or sometimes I pull or prune another five . . . or ten . . . or fifteen.

I realize that other gardeners work all day cleaning out a border and then start tidying up somewhere else the next day. I admire their persistence and single-mindedness. I wish I were like them.

But I am easily distracted. For instance, I just took a pail of kitchen scraps out to a pawpaw tree I had planted. I dumped the scraps a few inches from the little trunk, covered them with mulch, and stepped on the mulch to break down the scraps that are already becoming compost.

I had intended to come into the house immediately to write this chapter, but there was a briar encircling the pawpaw so I pulled it up. My inclination was to then check on the larkspur but, instead of doing that, I made myself pull up four more briars and then I pulled up another five.

Tired of eradicating briars, I went to look at the larkspur, thinned seedlings for five minutes, and then picked up five of the grapevine branches pruned by my husband. He is good at clipping but not picking up after himself. Isn't that a surprise?

Picking up my compost pail, I headed for the house by way of the back border where there were more weeds to pull and bare spots in need of mulch. I admired some dwarf veronica (*Veronica peduncularis* 'Georgia Blue'), just three inches tall and in full royal blue bloom, and thought how nice it would look under daffodils.

I dug up five little veronica plugs and replanted three where daffodils have emerged. I have trowels stuck all over the garden for occasions like this, firmly believing that plants should be divided when inspiration strikes and before memory fades.

After planting three veronicas, I potted up the other two tiny plants. I checked the tomato plants in the greenhouse, went to look for my compost pail that I had put down somewhere, and finally headed back to the word processor.

Now that I have introduced the Rule of Five, let me refer to an even handier Rule of Green Thumb: Gently cut back almost every single plant *after it blooms,* whether it is an annual, perennial, or shrub. Annuals and most perennials will rebloom. Even crepe myrtles rebloom if seedheads are removed.

With shrubs, pruning encourages new growth for next year's blossoms. For example, cut back azaleas when blooms fade and they will spend the summer growing leaves and setting buds in preparation for next spring. Cut them back in the fall or late winter and you will have nothing but foliage when neighbors' azaleas are heralding spring.

Cut back buddleia and lantana in early spring. Butterfly bushes (*Buddleia davidii*) should be cut back to about seven inches, even though by late February they are probably leafing out. This is a plant that becomes weedy if unpruned, and the blooms occur on new wood anyway.

In late winter or early spring, I cut the oldest stems of abelia and late-blooming spirea down to the ground (still sticking to the Rule of Five) and many of the other stems by half. Adhering to the Rule of Green Thumb, I trim early-blooming spireas this way *after* the flowers fade.

If you have hydrangeas that bloom on new wood, cut them to the ground in late winter. If you are not sure, leave them alone and be observant this year. Make notes on your calendar or in your journal about the blooming patterns, indicating whether they should be cut back in late winter or after they bloom this summer.

If foliage plants such as hollies, cleyera, and pittosporum are leggy and overgrown, cut them down to twelve to eighteen inches to re-shape them. You will make me happy if you pledge not to shear them into boxes, pyramids, or balls. Let shrubs grow as nature intends, trimming here and there, now and then, to keep them within bounds and shapely.

So much for garden rules. No penalty for breaking them . . . except the possibility of a year without blooms. You may lose a plant or two by dividing at the wrong time of year, but so what? Plants forgive much more readily than people, and they are easily replaced when we do them in.

Garden Smarter

Like most avid readers I clip items that I think will come in handy some day or that I plan to read when I get the time. Occasionally I pass these nuggets on to family and friends, but usually I file them away "for later."

Recently I took out a file to prepare a gardening program I call "Adapting to the Facts of Life." It is a topic I think about frequently since I am fast reaching the point when I must do some adapting myself.

Tucked in among the articles about ergonomic garden tools, stretching exercises, and posture was this neat little gem: An hour of swimming, weight training, or walking briskly uses 270 calories; an hour of gardening uses 340.

Here is more good news: An hour of housework uses a mere 180 calories. Hardly worth the bother. An hour of medium aerobics uses 395 calories and running five and a half miles, 588. In terms of calorie count, gardening may not be the champion, but I cannot think of a more pleasurable way to work off a piece of chocolate cake.

Of course, gardening does a whole lot more than use up calories. Unless you have turned your garden into a stress-creating project (and I have known gardeners who do this), you are well aware of your garden's therapeutic quality.

You cannot stay angry when immersed in the delights your garden provides, or at least I cannot. Fifteen minutes of dividing perennials to plant elsewhere or to share with friends, and I forget who or what provoked my ire.

Unless your brain is bigger than mine, you cannot think about your troubles or ponder the world's problems as you decide what to plant in that empty spot in midborder or as you clip the top of the hedge to give sunlight to the bottom.

Since I chose as my gardening role model a woman who died at 96, probably with shovel in hand, I am taking steps to ensure that I too will have my hands in the dirt long into my dotage.

Ruth Stout, the author of *How to Have a Green Thumb without an Aching Back,* toiled in the rocky soil of Connecticut and threw most of her effort into the cultivation of vegetables. For a year she ate only what she could eat raw. She occasionally gardened in the nude.

We differ on several counts. I am always clothed while outdoors, and most of my favorite foods are cooked. I regard Stout as my mentor because she taught me to compost by tucking vegetable peels and garden trimmings under the mulch rather than fooling with a labor-intensive compost pile. She taught me to mulch generously, with hay, leaves, newspaper, or other material, to deprive weed seeds of light and to conserve moisture.

She taught me to take life easy, to treasure the small delights of a garden, and to recognize the endless satisfaction to be garnered from a plot of ground. And, best of all, she taught me that I too could continue to do so all my life.

Here are a few steps I am taking to assure that I will never, in this lifetime, have to give up the pleasures of a garden. I mulch so I do not have to pull weeds. I try out tools before buying them to make sure they do not aggravate the arthritis in my thumbs or strain my shoulder muscles.

My husband and I just bought our first riding lawn mower, complete with leaf vacuum, because we know the day will come when pushing a mower is more than we can do, and raking our tree-filled yard is already too much of a chore.

An alternative is to hire someone else to mow and rake, and I would do this happily. However, I am married to a man who values independence beyond the point most folks consider reasonable. At 75, he still crawls under the car to change his oil to make sure it is done right. What more can I say?

But some tasks machines cannot do. You have to do them yourself. In doing these jobs, I make a point of varying my movements. I rake fifteen minutes and then do something else. I prune fifteen minutes and then pot up seedlings. I push the wheelbarrow while gathering pinecones, then I dig a few holes or pull up wayward ivy.

The point is to vary tasks so you change the stress on your body. Most aches and pains are caused by repetitive motions that continue too long. Limit the hardest jobs to brief periods. Complete them over days rather than in a single session. Of course, not doing them at all is an option.

Think in terms of growing in containers or having raised beds built. I have two friends, one with arthritis and the other a paraplegic, who garden successfully in raised beds they can reach across and tend comfortably.

As we grow older or experience physical ailments, we need not give up gardening. We need to garden smarter by cutting down the area we cultivate and by choosing plants that require less care. Hire someone to help. Buy machines that perform miracles.

Whatever accommodations you make, do not give up gardening or any other pastime that brings you joy or enhances your life. At 96, Ruth Stout was thinking about next spring, and we should do the same.

Getting Personal in the Garden

Not long ago I went on a tour of houses and gardens in a historic Southern city. Naturally I was more interested in gardens than home décor, but, in one of the houses, I noticed a framed quotation that caught my interest: "Show me your garden and I shall tell you what you are."

The author is Alfred Wustin, and I know nothing about him. I think the statement is presumptuous, but I sure know where Alfred was going with it. The choices we make for our gardens reflect our personalities. One choice after another distinguishes our garden from any other. Just as a painting is uniquely an artist's, a garden is (or should be) uniquely the gardener's, a sum of the creative choices he or she makes.

The question is, for whose pleasure is the garden created? If your garden is for the neighbors, passersby, the garden club, or someone other than yourself, then your best choice may be to hire a landscaper to do it for you. He or she will do it faster, more efficiently, and perhaps even more cheaply in the long run.

I see too many gardens that look as if they came from a kit, even when they were planned by the owners themselves. In fact, some of these impersonal and same-old, same-old gardens are in the aforementioned historic city, on tour! I assume Alfred would tell the owners they are bores or stodgy sticks-in-the-mud.

I hope readers of these pages can say with confidence, "This garden is mine. I make choices to delight myself. It is a mirror of my soul."

Once you establish that your garden is for you, think in terms of your own pleasures and habits. Do you want a garden that tests your perseverance, challenges you physically, makes your muscles ache? I have nothing to say to you, so you might as well stop reading.

Do you want a garden that is pleasurable to maintain? A joy to behold? A place to sit and ponder? A source of entertainment while standing at the sink? Do you want flowers for the house and for sharing with friends?

In other words, think about what you want your garden to do. A garden, if it is to mirror your soul, needs to enrich your life on a daily basis. It should be a good friend you want to visit often and to know intimately.

By all means, choose a location for your garden that invites frequent visiting. Not only does an appropriate location mean that you will see more of your garden, but you will also maintain it easily, pulling a weed here or clipping a spent bloom there as you stroll.

One of my first gardening efforts was a perennial border, a narrow strip in front of a hedge across the back of our acre lot. It might as well have been in my neighbor's yard. My next project was an herb garden, even farther away, closer to my neighbor's kitchen than to mine.

Needless to say, I used few herbs and the perennials were overtaken by weeds. This was before I began suppressing weeds with newspapers and mulch, but the basic problem was making dumb choices in locating my gardens.

If they had been closer to our house and on my daily route, I might have regularly pulled a few weeds, picked herbs for the pot, and enjoyed the day-by-day changes that gardens make.

Concentrate your efforts where you and your family will enjoy your garden most. I suggest you use two perspectives: one looking out from the house and another in the yard itself.

A garden I visited recently is a visual delight from the sunroom because the owners (who are in their eighties) made choices to fit their lifestyle. The sunroom is where they sit at every opportunity, and what a panorama they have outside those windows. Birds perch, butterflies pause, the garden itself basks in attention.

Your outdoor decision making should focus on an area (or areas) where you walk and sit. Have in mind a path for yourself and visitors. Create garden spaces that bring different pleasures. Put benches where you want guests to stop. Think of yourself as a theatrical director who not only designs the set but also moves the actors.

Except in the coldest climates, most of us are able to have attractive gardens all year, especially if we select plants with foliage that provides something interesting to look at, even when we have no flowers. The choices of foliage are more important (and usually less attended to) than the choices we make in flowers. Blooms come and go much too quickly, but even deciduous foliage lasts three seasons and evergreens are, well, always green.

Getting Personal in the Garden

But, even with a four-season garden, you need to choose a season or two when your garden is at its most spectacular (unless you have the staff and wherewithal of a botanical garden). Although most gardeners choose spring as their "best season," my own garden peaks in early fall. To achieve this autumn glory, I choose plants that bloom from late August until the first hard frost.

I find that spring takes care of itself since most perennials and annuals are in first flower and I am thrilled that winter is over. Everything is new. In fall, however, my garden is lush and excessive. Plants overlap and stems twist around, emerging through foliage of other plants. The garden is full of surprises.

Is it important to you that bloom colors coordinate with one another? Do you want serenity or pizzazz? Do you love chartreuse? Burgundy? Cool or hot? All white? The choices are yours . . . all of them. Keep in mind: None of the choices is necessarily permanent and none of them, not one, is so wrong it ruins a life.

The Grand Tourist

Chances are, if you are a gardener, you will be going on a garden tour or two this spring. I love garden tours, myself, whether I am visiting a neighbor's garden, a public garden, or a group of private gardens open for visitors on a particular day. A garden that is on tour is usually at its best, primped and primed for weeks for the occasion.

A friend of mine was coaxed into putting her garden on tour to benefit her local Master Gardener organization. She has worked for months, bypassing social events, good books, and who knows what else to get her garden ready for folks who will visit in April. This garden is always a treat to see, and I cannot wait to visit when it is all dressed up for the party. However, I am glad it is not my garden.

Occasionally gardens are open for touring any time. You will see small signs saying "Open Garden," and that means you are invited to drop in, walk around, and enjoy. Although I admire the concept, I would never have the nerve to do this myself.

I am not a neat person and am invariably in midproject somewhere in my garden. The thought that someone with high expectations could drop in at any time makes my stomach queasy. However, if people call and ask to come, I warn them what to expect and invite them to take their chances and come on over.

Here is what I like people to do in my garden. Enjoy it. Look for the nicest parts. Ask questions. Request cuttings or seeds but do not take without asking, please. I know it is done, and I have done it myself at times, but it is polite to ask.

I was visiting a garden once and leaned over to pull up a seedling struggling for life in the pathway, surely fair game for picking. The gardener was stunned by my audacity, and I have never made the mistake again, at least not in her garden or when the gardener was looking.

I will be impressed if you bring a notebook and write things down. It makes me a little nervous when people write down what I say, but I am also flattered by the trust it implies, as if the listener believes what

I am saying. If you want to take a picture, go ahead. I would be happy for you to remember what you enjoyed most.

Stay out of the borders unless invited in. The gardener knows where to step but you do not, and surely you do not want to walk on her prize seedlings or emerging bulbs.

Do not point out flaws. The gardener knows all about them and does not need reminding.

Here is a suggestion that may surprise you: Do not talk at length about your own garden. I know people who have toured the finest gardens of England and never stopped talking about the exquisite qualities of their own gardens back home.

You simply cannot focus on a garden the way it should be seen while you are thinking about your own. It is like looking at a museum masterpiece and thinking about the print above your sofa. It may be a fine print and match the sofa perfectly, but you have paid to look at the *Mona Lisa*, for heaven's sake.

My garden is not a masterpiece, but if you have come to see it and I am showing it to you, please hang in there with me and pretend to pay attention. Remember: You may be wishing for a cutting or two before you leave.

Do not talk to your friends while others are trying to hear about the plants. Last year some friends and I visited Montrose in Hillsborough, North Carolina. This is one of the best private gardens in the Southeast and the gardener, Nancy Goodwin, is a well-known plantswoman and writer. My friends and I had paid to visit her garden and listen to her talk as she guided us around.

Unfortunately, we were not alone. With us was what we thought was a garden club of high-heeled, and obviously well-heeled, ladies, some of whom chatted with one another throughout the tour. Annoyed looks from the rest of us left them unfazed. They yakked on. Actually, it turned out to be a book club and not a garden club at all. You would think literate women would realize Montrose was not their cup of tea and go back to their van and wherever they were going for lunch.

Benefit tours of private gardens are inspiring entertainment, and community organizations offer them in abundance. They are excellent fundraisers with minimal overhead (except for the garden owners). Gardens chosen for these tours are usually magnificently maintained, at least for the week or two before and after the tour, and have special features making them tour-worthy.

As you tour, look for plants that grow successfully in situations like your own. Notice how the garden is designed and organized. Are there places to sit? Do paths lead somewhere? Do you see the whole garden at once, or are there hidden niches and surprises? Does the garden reflect the personality of the owner? What plants edge the border? Is there a variety of color? Texture? Shapes?

Decide ahead of time what you want to pay attention to and you will see more as you stroll around, sort of like those study guides teachers hand out to keep overwhelmed students focused.

Enjoy the stroll. Ponder nature's delights. And don't forget your notebook.

The Grand Tourist

CHAPTER 2

Autumn

Make your garden a continual pleasure, stretching
your imagination as well as your muscles,
enriching your soul as well as the soil.

A Time of Renewal

It is no secret to gardening friends how much I love the fall land-scape. The rain, the cooler temperatures, and the energy that has lain dormant in both me and my plants combine to make this season second only to spring in gardening delight.

Like spring, autumn is a time of renewal. Many tasks await, but they are satisfying jobs that assure us future bounty and pleasure. For starters, if you have access to aged manure or compost, spread it now so it can rest over the winter months before going to work in the spring.

I continue to mulch with hay, pinestraw, and shredded leaves because I like the way mulch looks. Even though, in the climate where I garden, plants do not need protection from snow and ice, mulch helps keep the soil temperature stable on those odd winter days when temperatures rise.

And, of course, the mulch breaks down, enriching the soil's nutrients and texture. I scatter dolomitic lime throughout the borders and wherever I have anything planted, including the lawn. Lime requires months to break down but, when it does, it enables plants to absorb nutrients that would be wasted otherwise.

I occasionally spread kelp meal, alfalfa meal, or other organic amendments over the soil but, after years of mulching, my soil has become self-sufficient just as nature intends. Until your soil reaches this state of nirvana, put the bulk of your gardening budget into amendments, compost, manure, and mulch. A three-dollar plant will thrive in healthy soil, but a hundred-dollar plant will languish in poor soil. Remain patient and keep shoveling that compost. The most important soil improvement tool is a soil sample test.

Take at least a cup and a half of soil from various locations in the area you will be planting, put it in a jar or plastic bag, and take it to your local county agent's office. For a small fee, you will get a computer printout chock-full of information about the condition of your soil and what it needs.

As a result, you will be able to enrich your soil with nutrients it requires and will probably save money, purchasing only resources you need. I request organic recommendations, and you should too. However, if you want chemicals and numbers, the extension office will oblige.

If you plan to start a new bed or extend an old one (and what gardener doesn't?), place a layer of newspaper at least eight sheets thick over the area, top that with compost, and finally top with hay, pine-straw, or shredded leaves. The plot will be ready for planting next spring without the use of shovel, rake, or tiller.

If you intend to transplant trees or shrubs either from your own garden or someone else's (assuming you have permission), "root prune" them now and they will be ready to move in December or January when they are dormant. To root prune, take a sharp-edged shovel and slice deep into the soil in a circle around the trunk. Your circle should be *at least* halfway between the trunk and the branch line.

Root pruning encourages the plant to generate new feeder roots closer to the trunk area so, when you transplant it, you will also be transplanting a strong root system and the tree or shrub will have a much better chance of thriving in its new location. Be sure to flag the root-pruned plant if it is deciduous and your memory is like mine.

On the other hand, you can take your chances and dig up a tree or shrub whenever you decide it needs to be moved. I have done this myself oftener than I care to admit. Dig the hole at the new location and fill it with water. When the water has been absorbed, fill the hole with water again. When the soil is moist, put the plant, with as many roots as you can save, into the hole. Fill in with soil, water the surface thoroughly, and mulch.

I am frequently asked about drying herbs for winter use. Where I live, perennial herbs can be harvested year-round so there is no need to preserve them. The one exception is oregano since, unless dried, it tastes like grass. Rosemary, thyme, chives, sage, fennel, and parsley are better right out of the garden, and that is where I get mine.

If I lived in a cold climate, I would harvest herbs at their peak and dry them in the microwave oven. Although fresh herbs are sold year round now in grocery stores, they are expensive and have often been sitting around long enough to be no more flavorful than commercially dried herbs. Fresh is best but herbs from the garden, quickly dried and packaged, are a close second.

Basil, an annual that loses its will to live with the first heavy frost, loses its flavor when it is dried. To keep basil for winter cooking, you can freeze it in just enough water to cover. However, since basil is at its best in pesto, why not freeze it that way and you will be halfway to dinner as soon as it thaws? Like money in the bank.

It is a good idea to put markers on perennials that die back so you will know where to expect them as you begin planting in the spring. A detailed map or photographs of your garden are useful resources, but a well-marked garden does double duty. You can see what plants are there, and you are prevented from digging them up at inopportune times.

Remember to make your gardening a continual pleasure, stretching your imagination as well as your muscles, enriching your soul as well as the soil.

September Separates the Optimists

September is the month that separates optimists from pessimists when it comes to gardening. The optimist's spirit is renewed by slightly cooler weather and the promise of rain. The optimist feels an overwhelming urge to divide plants, clip cuttings to root, gather seeds, and start a cool weather crop of greens. The pessimists, on the other hand, let summer failures drain their spirits. For them, it is still too hot, too dry, too laborious.

I am in league with the optimists of the world, in the garden and anywhere else I happen to be. The optimist has the joy of anticipation and, if all goes well, fruition. The pessimist endures the misery of dread no matter how things turn out.

Already looking forward to next year's garden, I collect seeds of annuals and perennials that have thrived so I can repeat some of this year's triumphs at no cost. In a pill vial or coin envelope, I store dried seeds of fennel, melampodium, zinnias, cypress vine, and other non-hybridized plants with obligingly easy-to-harvest seeds.

I make sure the seedhead is fully dry. It should be brown and crisp and ready to shatter. I rub the seedhead gently to separate seeds from chaff. I perform this satisfying task over newspaper and then let the seeds sit for a day or two indoors where it is cool and dry. I write on the container the kind of seeds and the year. I think I will remember, but I know spring is months away. I keep these seed packets in the refrigerator but doubt a location this cool is necessary.

As soon as things slow down in the garden, I begin thinking about spring and start columbine seeds. I love the cheery red and yellow native *Aquilegia canadensis,* supposedly an enthusiastic reseeder but not in my garden, perhaps because of my mulching habit. The columbine I really love, though, is the eye-stopping, rainbow-colored, thirty inch-tall *A.* 'McKana's Giant.'

Though columbine is a hardy perennial, it has a reputation for being short-lived and I worry about it disappearing from my garden. To allay my fear and provide me with an ever-expanding crop of

'McKana's Giants,' I start seeds every year. A packet of seeds is about two dollars. In the spring, a single plant will cost three dollars. Even I can do this math.

Mushroom containers are my favorite flats for starting seeds. I pierce the bottom with an ice pick (for drainage) and fill the flat to the top with moistened vermiculite or seed-starting mix. I sow the seeds over the surface without covering them. Then I place the flat in a plastic bag and put it in the refrigerator for a three-week vacation.

Next I place the flat somewhere warm and in a few weeks the columbine seedlings emerge. As soon as the first one emerges, I get the entire flat under light or in the sunniest location in my house, keeping the vermiculite moist but uncovered.

When seedlings have formed true leaves, I dump the flat over, gently separate the small plants, and pot them up in individual containers filled with potting mix (not garden soil). I move them outdoors during a warm period and leave them there. They are small, but they are hardy perennials and expect to spend the winter outdoors. In the spring, I have dozens of columbines for my garden. You can too, all for the price of a seed packet.

I sow lettuce seeds outside in large shallow containers near the kitchen, harvesting leaves when they are four or five inches tall. I fill the container with potting mix enriched with mushroom or homemade compost, scatter seeds over the top, and water gently. In a few days seedlings emerge and, within a month, they become salad.

The advantage of growing lettuce this way is that you can move the pots to shelter young plants from hot sun or hard rains. A lettuce crop makes an attractive container garden, especially if you use a combination of leaf colors and textures. For the price of a head of tasteless grocery store lettuce, you can purchase a packet of mesclun mix seeds or buy several packets of greens and do your own mixing.

If you are a gardener who plants a winter crop of broccoli, collards, onions, turnips, and winter squash, I tip my sun hat to you. I am all in favor of growing more edibles, and in my next life I plan to do it.

Continue to deadhead annuals and perennials to keep them blooming. Cut off spent flowers and you will be pleasantly surprised by marigolds, petunias, and other plants that produce a final flush of blooms before succumbing to hard frost.

Speaking of annuals, if you live where pansies are planted in fall, for the widest choice and best plants, purchase flats as soon as you see them. Get the pansies planted in a sunny spot before they bloom, when roots are fresh and uncrowded. Fertilize occasionally with liquid or granular fertilizer, and you will be blessed with blooms through the next three seasons.

I plant pansies on top of daffodil bulbs so that in early spring daffodils emerge through a bed (or pot) of blooming annuals. This is easy to accomplish but surprisingly impressive to less resourceful folks.

Garden centers get sharper every year about stocking perennials in the fall, which is the way it should be. The best time to plant perennials in zones seven to ten is in the fall so roots have all winter to establish themselves before summer, our toughest season.

If you have overcrowded perennials in your garden, divide them now. The general rule is to divide spring perennials in fall and summer perennials in spring, but I say divide when the urge strikes.

If you have neglected the birds over the summer, start feeding them again and continue to provide fresh water. Do some research on different food combinations. You will be richly rewarded by the variety of birds attracted to your feeder and the continuing pleasure of their company.

27

Autumn Joys

What is pink, insect-free, hardy as the dickens, and blooms in September? I can think of three answers to this query and confidently vouch for the entire trio: *Anemone xhybrida* (Japanese anemone), *Sedum* 'Autumn Joy,' and *Chrysanthemum xmorifolium* 'Ryan's Pink.' For gardeners who think spring is the be-all in the border, add these to your garden and fall will take on a whole new look.

It is not easy to find a breath of spring in September and October, but Japanese anemones put me in mind of April breezes and the fresh scent of May. The lobed green leaves serve as an attractive but unassuming groundcover all summer and then, in late August, tinted buds emerge on the tips of two- or three-foot-long wiry stems.

In a few days, the buds burst into pink, mauve, dark rose, or white single, semidouble, or double blooms. With about a dozen cultivars of Japanese anemone on the market, if you plant an assortment, you can keep the show going from late August to frost.

The flowers are two or three inches across with a center clump of gold stamens. They look like butterflies at the tips of slender stems, leaning across the border as if checking out the neighbors. Every breeze catches them, causing them to bob and bounce like small kites.

Until recently, I had no idea that Japanese anemones do not like to be moved or divided. Last spring I wanted some of these beauties in places other than my shady island border, so I dug up small rooted sideshoots and tucked them here and there according to whim. As far as I can tell, they survived and thrived, which just goes to show that ignorance really can be bliss.

Japanese anemones like well-drained, fertile soil with plenty of organic material mixed in. Filtered sunlight is ideal, but in my yard they grow in both full and dappled shade and seem content where they happen to be. If you are going to follow the rules, think before you plant so you will not have to move them. On the other hand, do not hesitate to move a clump if you decide it would be happier elsewhere.

They take a few years to become established, but you will have a few flowers the first year and more every year after that. Some gardeners complain about the tendency of Japanese anemones to spread. But those are the folks who complain about everything that wanders from its assigned place, so do not let their whining discourage you.

Make a note on the March page of your calendar to seek out Japanese anemones. Spring is when you will find them in the garden center. Unlike most perennials, spring is the best time to plant Japanese anemones and, judging from my personal experience, to dig them up and move them.

Sedum 'Autumn Joy' has a quite different look. Nothing bouncy or sylph-like about this beauty, which grows about two feet tall and eighteen inches wide. 'Autumn Joy' has fleshy pale green foliage and dense velvety domes of tiny blooms, like pink broccoli. The color changes over the summer from cream to pale pink to rose, rust, and, just before frost, mahogany, a fancy word for brown.

Unlike Japanese anemone, sedums tolerate drought and prefer less fertile soil and plenty of sunlight. They grow in shade or semishade but tend to fall over. To avoid this floppiness, I pinch 'Autumn Joy' back to four or five inches when they reach about eight inches in height. However, this results in smaller blooms so, if it is size you are after, you may want to leave them unpinched and floppy.

I use 'Autumn Joy' in flower arrangements, where they last a long time and add interesting fuzzy texture to the mix. Do not cut off the blooms for any other reason, however. Let them dry on their stems and use them in arrangements or spray them gold or silver to use as Christmas ornaments.

All sedums are easy to propagate from stem or leaf cuttings, or you can lift the entire plant early in spring when it emerges and divide it every three or four years. *Chrysanthemum xmorifolium* 'Ryan's Pink' is another fall bloomer that, like Japanese anemone, sits quietly all summer without complaint about drought or heat. Then, as the weather cools, buds begin to form and, by October, you have a mass of three-inch pink daisies with butter-yellow centers.

Happiest in sun, 'Ryan's Pink' will also bloom in partial shade. My plants flop over and crawl around, working their way through the foliage of other plants. A newer form of hardy chrysanthemum is 'Country Girl,' which I understand has even more abundant pink blooms and sturdier foliage and stems. I would have said 'Ryan's Pink' was as good as a gardener could get but, in horticulture, improvements never cease. 'Ryan's Pink' can be divided or propagated from cuttings just about any time. A friend was planning an outdoor wedding reception in mid-October. I made about fifty cuttings for her in June so they would be ready to party (in the pink, so to speak) when the wedding bells rang.

If you pine for a garden that keeps on giving, add fall-blooming perennials that come into their own as days and nights cool down. Why deny yourself a three- or four-season garden, especially when it requires so little labor and bestows such abundance?

Keep Your Eyes on the Groundcovers

Groundcovers get short shrift in the gardening world. In the first place, they are down there at ground level, where they are supposed to be, and as a result do not get noticed much by casual viewers. They are unstately, as a rule, and used in mass rather than as individual specimens.

Groundcovers serve as background (or underground) for other plants, not terribly distinctive in their own right but attractive layering, much like a mat around a photograph. Their basic job is to suppress weeds and to serve as living mulch, but they also enhance larger upright plants.

In my garden, ferns pop up through variegated lamium. Tropical-looking chameleon plant (*Houttuynia cordata*) surrounds hydrangeas, and creeping raspberry (*Rubus calycinoides*) meanders under daphne and fatsia. The variegation of the lamium sets off the dark woodland greens of the vertical ferns. Chameleon plant adds silky texture under the large coarse hydrangea leaves, but not so much color that it detracts from the blooms. The crinkled leathery foliage of creeping raspberry underscores the smooth glossy leaves of daphne and fatsia.

Under an enormous magnolia tree next to our house is a solid mass of variegated *Vinca major*, a stoloniferous evergreen perennial that seems indestructible. Years ago, my husband limbed up this magnolia in a fit of obsessive neatness. For a year, thick, barely biodegradable leaves fell, making an unattractive mess. Of course, grass in this shade was out of the question. One day I saw vinca growing *under* a beach house and thought such a shade-lover would grow under my magnolia tree. Sure enough. In no time, I had a bountiful crop that covered the entire shadow of the magnolia, lighting up the area and covering up those leaves.

Not only do groundcovers suppress weeds and provide shade to the soil, but they also offer shelter as well as food to lizards, toads, earthworms, and other beneficial small creatures. Remember, we are all in this together, and we should make the entire food chain feel welcome and comfortable.

Groundcovers provide hunting ground and entertainment for small ground birds. The squirrels like them for storing nuts, and voles and moles do not tunnel under groundcovers, at least in my yard. They do not tunnel anywhere else, either, so I suspect our schnauzer and Labrador retriever deter rodents more than the groundcovers do.

Groundcovers can replace grass and often should. I do not know why we struggle to get grass to grow where it is obviously not happy, when we could plant any number of textured groundcovers such as pachysandra, ivy, mondo grass, or ferns that would flourish.

Unlike other plant groups that can be neatly defined, groundcovers are a nebulous group. A tree or vine has a distinctive growth habit. So does a shrub or a fern. But groundcovers can be shrubs or ferns or grasses or vines.

For instance, under a crepe myrtle, I grow a mass of Siberian iris that bloom in spring and look like strappy grass until frost. They behave as a groundcover though I think of them as perennials. Low-growing junipers and cotoneasters, or even hip-high junipers and cotoneasters, are effective groundcovers under trees and large shrubs.

A friend who has a steep dry bank without irrigation asked me what he could plant there. I suggested northern oats (*Chasmanthium latifolium*), a grass that looks like sea oats but is very green except during winter. Northern oats move gently in the wind and are a sight to behold. They are also incredibly tough, survive drought conditions, and spread. Boy, do they spread, which is just what my friend wanted them to do.

Vines, grasses, hostas, sedums, ferns, and shrubs can all be found in lists of groundcovers simply because they can, and often do, spread out and cover areas of ground. Herbs such as creeping thyme and oregano make excellent and flavorful groundcovers in the sun. Sweet woodruff (*Galium odoratum*) provides the same service in shade and is the raw material for May wine.

The key to turning a plant into a groundcover is to plant enough of them so they close ranks and become a solid mass. Your best bet for getting a groundcover started is to remove or kill any grass or weeds, preferably with newspaper and mulch put down a few months earlier. When the grass is gone or dead, set out the plants and keep the soil moist until you see new growth. Then stand back and watch your groundcover flow like lava over the soil.

Because they were born to spread, groundcovers require a watchful eye or they might take over the world like that ultimate groundcover, kudzu. In front of my house and in one section of my back garden I have a crop of English ivy, which someone gave me as a single uprooted plant almost forty years ago. Supposedly it is a descendent of ivy growing in Anne Hathaway's garden at Stratford-on-Avon.

In spite of its fancy ancestor, this ivy has become a thug, growing up trees and shrubs as well as the house. Anne Hathaway expected ivy to grow on her cottage, but my husband is not happy to see it creep upward on the brickwork.

Ivy is a super plant—attractive, tough, and long-lived—but it does take management. When I planted mine I had small children and, a few years later, a job and a second house where we spent most of the summer. The ivy did what it was supposed to do but I did not, and I still have not gotten a grip on it.

The same is true of variegated vinca, which I planted with such success under the magnolia tree. I also planted it in the wrong place, near my long mixed border, where it continues to appear no matter what I do to eradicate it. This just goes to show that a gardener needs to stay on her toes and pick plants and locations wisely.

I am fascinated by groundcovers and use them lavishly, perhaps even excessively. Many homeowners, especially those whose goal is minimal maintenance, prefer to use mulching materials in lieu of spreading plants. I use both and, if an enthusiastic groundcover grows right over the mulch, I say, more power to it.

Mixing It Up in the Border

We gardeners love perennials and for good reason. They appreciate our attention enough to show up the following year and continue to return year after year through drought, downpours, and freezes. They are the hardy guys, and we would all do well to emulate their resilience and perseverance.

If you are starting a new perennial bed, or reviving an old one, dig in as much compost as you have or can afford to buy. Add kelp meal or other organic soil amendments, including dolomitic lime. Do not mix in fertilizer or manure at this time. In late winter or early spring, when top growth starts peeking out from the mulch, scatter it on the surface. That is when plants need nitrogen.

After twenty years, my perennial border has morphed happily into a "mixed border." It is well established and I do not intend to expand it more than a few inches here, a few there, when my husband (who thinks we need more grass and fewer flowers) is elsewhere.

My goal is to fluff up a section every year. The section might be six to ten feet, crowded with an assortment of perennials, ferns, herbs, perhaps a shrub or two, and even a small tree. My border is exuberantly diverse as a mixed border should be.

On a warmish fall day, ideally a day or two before rain, I remove the perennials and other diggable plants from the chosen section and either wrap them in wet newspaper or divide and pot them up. I dig up only shrubs that need to be moved to some other location. I remove the mulch, fork up the soil if it is compacted, add soil amendments, and dig again.

Let me assure you I am not talking about "double digging." This is a peculiar type of torture in which the gardener digs down a foot and removes the soil, digs another foot, and puts the topsoil into the bottom and the bottom soil on top. I am not making this up. There are well-intentioned gardeners who actually do this.

Personally, I want my best soil in the top eight to twelve inches of the soil, just as nature does it. I remove mulch, distribute whatever amendments I want over the soil, and mix the area up without removing the soil or digging any deeper than the roots will be absorbing nutrients.

Then I replant the best of the old divided perennials (after trimming their roots and foliage a bit), and add new plants as well as divisions I have taken from other areas of the garden.

I do not initially plant large drifts of varieties as knowledgeable garden designers advise us to do. Budget constraints force me to purchase one plant of this and one plant of that and propagate more of each to drift with sometime in the future.

However, even after I have gone forth and multiplied, I prefer to repeat plants throughout the garden so I can admire my favorites in a variety of settings, like seeing good friends often rather than once or twice a year.

Remodeling a section of the garden is a whole lot more fun than cleaning out the attic. Both jobs are satisfying when they are over, but when you redo a garden, you follow a dream. When you clean out an attic or a closet, all you do is get rid of some junk and keep more than you should.

In a garden renovation, everything that can be moved easily, including bulbs, gets dug up, divided, rearranged, replanted, or potted up. At the end of this labor, I am a rich woman indeed. I have a renewed garden plot and many extra plants to share. If rain is not imminent, I water well to get everything settled, mulch the plot with hay or shredded leaves, and look forward to spring.

A cautionary note: Experts recommend dividing spring-blooming perennials in fall and fall-blooming plants in the spring. That makes sense but I divide when the mood strikes, knowing full well that it may not strike again for a decade (though this is more apt to happen with the attic than the garden).

In fact, I do not divide only when I am renovating part of the border. As I take my daily morning stroll, I pounce on plants that look as if they need to be separated.

For instance, just the other day I found *Patrinia scabiosifolia* almost hidden behind a shrub that had expanded over the summer. Around the base of the butter-yellow patrinia were a dozen baby plants that could be eased out of the soil or clipped from the mother plant. I shared a few with friends, potted some for a plant sale, and replanted the rest where they would get plenty of sun.

Mixing It Up in the Border

Other perennials that are easily divided this way are veronicas, salvias, stokes aster, daisies, solidago, rudbeckia, chrysanthemums, and sedums. Just ease the little rooted plants that appear around the base out of the soil or dig up the whole plant and pull it apart gently.

And, by all means, select a new perennial to perk up the garden come spring. Not long ago we could not find perennials for fall planting, but that is no longer true. We have all learned a lot and, as we urge local nurseries to keep the perennials coming, our gardens continue to grow and so do we.

When the Tough Get Going

I am always surprised when I hear accomplished gardeners complain about the way their gardens look in the fall. I think my own garden is at its best, at its lushest and most luxuriant, in the month of October.

Fall brings rain, days are warm but nights are cool, and plants that have limped through a hot dry summer have, at last, come into their own and are flourishing. Just like people, plants are often improved by having to tough out tough times.

October wears a golden aura with swamp sunflowers (*Helianthus angustifolius*) finally getting their deserved attention after reaching six to eight feet in height, joined by rudbeckia, chrysanthemums, and, of course, the much maligned goldenrod.

Nothing beats a field of goldenrod or *Solidago spp.* for pure glory, unless it is a field of rape, the source of canola oil, in the Cotswolds. When I was in England, a British friend was embarrassed by all that gold. Its brilliance seemed "unEnglish" to her eye. "Not quite right for us," she whispered. "Too yellow."

We crass Americans loved those sun-drenched fields. Flashy is Us! Goldenrod deserves the same admiration if we just forget the myth that it makes us sneeze. (It is ragweed that brings on the snorts and happens to bloom at the same time.)

Solidago flourishes in untended fields because it is drought-tolerant. Native solidago spreads by runners and seed, which explains those masses of gold, but the hybrids in our borders are more manageable clump formers.

In my own garden, back by the hedge, I have a loosely formed solidago that must be close to five feet tall by the end of the season. In the middle of the border I grow *S. rugosa* 'Fireworks' topping out at three feet, and in the front is *S. sphacelata* 'Golden Fleece,' which sits quietly through summer but in early September achieves stardom in the garden and blooms for at least a month.

The foliage of 'Golden Fleece' is around eight inches tall, but the prostrate branches are fifteen to eighteen inches of pure gold. You might never notice 'Golden Fleece' in a field, but it sure adds panache in a border or flower arrangement.

Contrary to the rule that fall perennials should be divided in the spring, I divide 'Golden Fleece' and several other perennials right after they bloom since that is when I think about them. I like to do this job and all my transplanting after a soaking rain. It seems logical that roots will be less stressed after a relaxing bath and will settle in for the winter, ready to burst forth vigorously in the spring. Just like me.

But gardeners do not live by perennials alone. A mixed border should have its share of annuals for continual color and interest.

Where I garden, pansies and violas will always dominate the late fall and winter landscape when it comes to color. I plant mine in late October to mid-November, and I prefer to purchase plants that are not yet blooming.

Although it is reassuring to see blossoms, annuals that are already blooming in their six-packs tend to be rootbound. Purchasing bloomless plants is an act of faith, though I have never been averse to surprises in the garden or anywhere else.

But height and texture must come from some source other than pansies and, luckily, winter vegetables can supply both, as well as vibrant color and vitamins. Giant red mustard, Swiss chard, curly green mustard, red kale, and parsley perk up my garden considerably during the winter months.

Winter greens (and reds) will look gorgeous to you as the world turns beige, so do not hide them in the vegetable garden. Tuck them into the mixed border, in containers, or among foundation shrubs where their colors and textures can be appreciated. They will thrive through winter and into spring until you are ready to grow something else.

I start winter vegetables from seed in mid-August so by early November the plants are ready to go in the ground. The trick is to have seeds on hand and a note on the August page of your calendar, reminding you that fall is approaching. I know from experience how hard it is to believe when the temperature is 100 plus.

As for summer annuals that are kaput, I cut them off at ground level or I let them die a natural death and regard them as on-the-spot compost. I leave perennials unpruned until early spring or until I cannot stand their shabbiness another day.

Remember to keep feeders and birdbaths full for migrants and residents. Enjoy your garden and share your bounty with those who share this earth.

Bulbs Predict a Glorious Spring

Gardeners are always in forward motion. No sooner do night temperatures dip into the thirties, reminding us to check the furnace and take in the houseplants, than we start pondering spring. Ahhh, spring, the season that keeps a gardener young and hopeful as she gets out her checkbook and picks up a bulb catalog.

Frugal as I am, I go first class when buying bulbs. I look for the biggest, fattest bulbs in the bins when buying locally. When ordering by mail, I buy from reputable dealers who specialize in bulbs. Forget those bargain bags of scrawny little bulbs that either will never bloom or will bloom once and then expire. Better to break open the wallet than to break one's heart.

When I began gardening twenty years ago, I ordered a "naturalizing collection" of varied narcissus from a topnotch nursery whose prices for plants are often shocking. Those bulbs bloomed the first year, and they and their offspring still put on a fabulous show beginning in late February and continuing into April. Now that is what I call a bargain.

Last spring, after the foliage fell over, beige and tired, I dug up a couple of groups of daffodil bulbs that had multiplied themselves into a mob scene. I let them dry out in the shade for a couple of days and then put them in the refrigerator where they are still resting. I could have replanted the separated bulbs immediately, but I was busy and thought they would enjoy a summer in the fridge.

Next spring, I fully intend to dig up and separate overcrowded daffodils as soon as their blooms fade. I know, I know. I am supposed to let the foliage die down, but past experience tells me I will no longer be interested in daffodils in May and I will have forgotten where I want to put them.

Since bulbs, once planted, remain in place for a long duration, it is well worth the time and effort to make the soil right. Good drainage is the key. Isn't it always? Dig the planting area to a depth of at least eight inches since the roots go down and the foliage goes up and you want to make the soil bulb-friendly in both directions.

I like to see daffodils grown in drifts rather than lined up in rows or planted singly. They make an impressive impact this way and, when the foliage dies down, you know more or less where they are and can overplant with summer annuals. Or, once you plant the bulbs, you can overplant immediately with pansies. In spring, daffodils and hyacinths pop up through the pansies and look fabulous.

Bulbs are divided into two groups. Major bulbs include narcissus (daffodils and jonquils), tulips, hyacinths, and crocus. Tulips have never rebloomed in my Southern garden, so I do not plant them and get my fill instead at a nearby botanical garden where they plant thousands and toss them after they bloom. I could never do such a thing myself.

I love all the narcissus, from the giant 'King Alfreds' to the miniature 'Tete-a-tetes.' I cannot imagine having too many daffodils and wish I had a field full of them. I especially enjoy seeing daffodils popping up around deserted houses along country roads, still greeting spring after years of neglect, exquisite symbols of resilience and self-sufficiency.

The minor bulbs include grape hyacinths, just six inches tall and usually blue; glory-in-the-snow (*Chinodoxa luciliae*); scillas; snowdrops *(Galanthus nivalis)*; and bulbous iris. Dwarf iris produce six-inch-tall lavender flowers in February and March, and the taller Dutch iris bloom in late April. The latter make especially fine cut flowers, like understated orchids in yellow, blue, purple, white, and bronze. I wish I had a field of these, too.

Once you have loosened your soil, incorporate fertilizer into the area. I use specific bulb fertilizer, an organic mix of cricket manure, rock phosphate, bone meal, blood meal, dolomitic limestone, granite meal, and compost. It is pricey, but I am using it in a limited area only once every five to six years.

A cheaper recommendation is five pounds of 20 percent superphosphate per 100 square feet, or one teaspoon per hole. When I first started gardening, bone meal was the fertilizer of choice and, although it is no longer recommended, it worked well for me until I decided to get fancier.

Whenever I redo a section of my garden, which involves stripping it of most plants, I incorporate plenty of compost to hold moisture

Bulbs Predict a Glorious Spring

and nutrients. Otherwise, I just move around my borders spreading compost and mulch on top of the soil. I shovel it around shrubs and perennials and let nature take its course.

The general rule is to plant bulbs at a depth that is twice their height. In other words, if a bulb is two inches from top to bottom, place that bottom four inches below the soil line. Plant tulips, daffodils, and hyacinths six inches deep. Plant grape hyacinths and crocus three inches deep.

Get spring bulbs in the ground before Thanksgiving, though I have planted as late as New Year's Day and, a few months later, was greeted by bright yellow blooms that will always be the essence of spring.

❧

42

Good Things Come in Small Bulbs

Some of the most treasured plants in our gardens are downright petite and we love them that way. Violets, epimediums, and forget-me-nots delight us. Small bulbs produce equally delightful flowers. These bulbs take up little room and, until they astonish us with unannounced blooms, they tend to be forgotten.

A couple of years ago, a friend gave me a sack of wrinkled brown corms for my November birthday. Never mind which birthday it was. The corms or tubers were fall-blooming *Cyclamen hederifolium*. I planted the odd little chunks in my shady island, which is a mix of shrubs, ferns, perennials, a clothesline now covered in autumn clematis, and a large hickory tree.

I am enthralled by these tubers that produce a bevy of four-inch-tall flowers like pink butterflies perched on wiry reddish-brown stems. As the blooms shrivel with age, as we all do, the stems corkscrew their way to ground level, seeds drop, and ants carry them off to other locations where the seeds become tubers. But that is not the end of the story. Ivy-like leaves, dark green with grayish mottling, emerge and remain as handsome winter foliage.

Cyclamen tubers do not multiply or produce offsets. Each individual tuber swells in size, producing an increasing crop of blooms (and seeds) every year. New tubers should be planted just an inch or two deep.

Cyclamen like shade and alkaline soil, so I give them a dose of lime once or twice a year at the same time I lime hellebores. My soil tends to be acidic, so I mark all plants that need extra liming with a top layer of pebbles to remind me to do so.

Do not confuse *Cyclamen hederifolium* with the tender house-plant, *C. persicum*. *C. hederifolium* (as well as *C. coum*, which has rounded leaves) is hardy in zones six to ten, maybe even zone five.

Cyclamen devotees owe a debt to Nancy Goodwin of Hillsborough, North Carolina. She fell in love with cyclamen on a trip to England decades ago and started collecting them. When she realized that cyclamen species were being depleted by unscrupulous scavengers, so she began raising tubers from seeds and selling them through her now-defunct Montrose Nursery.

I have been to Goodwin's garden, Montrose, several times but never in fall. It must be a sight with cyclamen varieties planted in every shady place. Now that I have discovered the charms of this diminutive plant, I will be looking for them everywhere and already have a trip to Montrose marked on next October's calendar.

Another recent horticultural discovery for me is zephyranthes or "rain lilies." Rain lilies grow out of clumps of reedy foliage that sit idly until a good shower occurs. Within a day or two, delicate six-petaled blooms, less than a foot tall, shoot upward out of the foliage. Somehow these little lilies know the difference between rain and a hose-soaking.

Zephyranthes candida has white blooms and is the toughest of the species, producing seeds as well as multiplying. *Z. grandiflora* has somewhat larger deep rose blooms and seems to be the most frequently cultivated. *Z. citrina,* which produces scented yellow blooms and lots of seeds, is the hardiest against cold and most tolerant of drought.

Zephyranthes are not fussy about soil conditions and will grow happily for years in sand or clay and even in bog gardens. They can be purchased as bulbs or growing in pots and, while they may skip a year or two after planting, just when the gardener has given up, they emerge.

On a recent trip to a charming woodland garden and bird sanctuary, I was reminded that lycoris is a flower undeservedly overlooked. I myself had never grown them but intend to make up for lost time. Lycoris (commonly called "naked ladies" because of their leafless stems) bloom in late summer and are best planted under deciduous trees where they will get winter sun and summer shade.

Always on the lookout for plants that will bloom in my shady island, I have ordered a dozen *Lycoris squamigera,* which are hardier and have larger blooms than the red spider lily, *L. radiata.* Next fall, I anticipate stems of *L. squamigera* to rise magically, followed by lilac-pink blooms about two feet tall. The blooms make excellent cut flowers.

L. squamigera has several common names besides 'naked ladies,' so you will hear them referred to as autumn amaryllis or, because of their overnight emergence, resurrection lilies, surprise lilies, and

44

magic lilies. Whatever you call them, they multiply quickly and, after blooming, produce winter foliage that disappears in spring.

Plant both *L. squamigera* and *L. radiata* bulbs six to eight inches deep and six to eight inches apart. The plants spread into clumps, which can be divided in spring every five or six years after the foliage goes into decline. Just remove the offsets and replant the mother plant and offspring where you want them.

My fondness for cyclamen, zephyranthes, and lycoris in no way diminishes my passion for daffodils. A gardener's heart expands to love every plant in her garden, especially those currently in bloom. What luck that we do not have to choose. In our gardens we can, and should, have it all.

Good Things Come in Small Bulbs

The Great Cover-Up

As we thoughtfully browsed at a community plant sale, a fellow shopper asked me about vines for a fence. She recalled something I had written on this topic after visiting a friend who has a long and enviable fence around a large town property.

Since vines are among my favorite living things, the question made me salivate just pondering the possibilities. I envisioned a black iron fence, a wooden picket fence, or, at the very least, a row of stout weathered wooden rails. To get my visual image focused, I asked her what kind of fence she had.

"A cyclone fence," she answered glumly. I could see that she too wished we were pondering something more picturesque.

My imagination quickly changed gears and switched from lush vines gracefully draped over wrought iron to hardy foliage that would provide quick and complete coverage. On a positive note, a cyclone fence, which no one regards as a thing of beauty, certainly provides substantial support for vines. It also keeps dogs in . . . or out, depending upon your intent.

Every garden has secrets to hide. Though we gardeners appreciate them, a thriving compost pile, utilitarian garden shed, plastic greenhouse, or overloaded potting table tend to be unsightly.

But, for most of us, it is not our own stuff that bothers us. It is the neighbors' yards that are eyesores or distractions, at least to our way of thinking. Alas, few of us have the much-to-be-desired "borrowed vistas" of mountain scenery, green pastures, or woodlands to enhance our personal landscapes.

Fortunately, we can screen what we do not want in view, not only hiding the unsightly but also focusing on the garden space we want to show off.

Across the back of our acre suburban lot is a hedge of dark green privet (*Ligustrum japonicum*). While I clip it to control its width since my mixed border runs in front of it, I let the hedge get as tall as it wants so that it gives us privacy as well as abundant cover and nesting area for birds.

Until eight years ago, we had a hedge of the ubiquitous and disease-prone red tips (*Photinia fraseri*). Tired of spraying for and griping about leafspot, which decimated the shrubs no matter what noxious treatment was applied, we did away with them. Recently I have noticed in my travels stands of perfectly healthy red tips. I wonder if these remaining shrubs have developed leafspot resistance as a result of decreased usage or if they are a graphic example of survival of the fittest.

Nevertheless, we cut our red tips to the ground and planted privet, a utilitarian, unspectacular shrub though, to its credit, it has creamy white blooms in late spring and black drupes or "berries" in the fall. Its job is to provide privacy and to serve as a background for the mixed border that, if I do say so myself, is a remarkable sight.

Ligustrums or other fast-growing evergreen shrubs would cover my friend's cyclone fence more dependably than vines. If I were using the hedge as a background for a mixed border, I would plant a single cultivar to serve as a wall of green to frame the garden, just as I did in my own yard.

However, if I were not planning a border in front of the hedge, I would plant a variety of shrubs to create what landscape designers call "a tapestry hedge." Not only would a mixed hedge be more interesting, but it would also provide insurance in case one kind of shrub lapsed into a coma sometime in the future. Much easier and cheaper to replant a few shrubs than to replace a whole row of expired red tips as we did.

One of my sons lives in a golf course community. When he installed an attractive, well-constructed wooden swing set in the backyard for our grandchildren, he received a snippy letter of complaint from the club's management. They not only wanted him to screen the play area from the sensitive eyes of golfers but also to change the color of the canopy from yellow to green. Go figure.

Since he decided it would be too much trouble to move or go to court, I suggested he plant a screen of ligustrums or viburnums that would fill in quickly so golfers' sensitivities would not be jarred and our grandchildren could play with relative abandon.

If you are in the market for evergreen shrubs for background or screening, check lists of specimens appropriate for your area and site conditions. Hedges should be reliable. They may be utilitarian, but they are long-term investments. You do not want to waste money and years by selecting something cheap but iffy.

But back to the cyclone fence. If it were in my yard, even if I planted a hedge, that fence would spend summer clothed in gourd vines. I would plant bumpy, oddly shaped, and multicolored decorative gourds, set up a kiosk in the fall, and become a millionaire in no time. If you have purchased gourds at the grocery store recently, you know what I mean.

I would also plant a mix of hardy evergreen vines such as one of the ivies, akebia, autumn clematis, cross vine, creeping fig, Carolina yellow jessamine, Asian jasmine, or confederate jasmine. Like the tapestry hedge, mixing up the vines (and adding annuals in the spring) makes a more interesting fence-line and you are not up the creek if one variety meets its demise.

You can screen an unsightly object or area with a fence panel or boxing. My husband built a three-sided box for our air conditioning unit out of lattice and four-by-fours. I grow clematis and annual vines up the lattice and hang a hayrack planter from the top edge. You can still hear the air conditioner, but at least it is out of sight.

Now, if I can just think of some way to hide the boat, truck, and ATV that clutter our backyard. Kudzu comes to mind . . . which just goes to show that, where there is a gardener's will, there is always a way.

Love Those Loropetalums

I did not know whether to laugh or to cry. Pulling into the drug store parking lot, I could not believe I was looking at a row of loropetalums cut into precise squares. What demon drives a man or woman to pick up clippers and chop away at a shrub blessed with a gracefully relaxed natural form until it looks like a twiggy cube?

Loropetalum chinense is a relatively new arrival on the American horticultural scene. A friend asked me about them recently, saying he had never seen them until a year or two ago and all of a sudden he is seeing them everywhere. He is right. A decade ago, loropetalums were almost unknown, but they are currently the darling of the nursery trade, and for good reason.

The natural shape of loropetalums is a mound of arching branches. Leaf color ranges from light green to deep burgundy, and the flowers, which appear in early spring, are white to deep pink. Until I saw a full-grown fifteen-foot green loropetalum with white blooms in a friend's garden, I wondered why anyone would choose green over burgundy. Now I want both . . . and why not?

Related to witch hazel, loropetalums were first found in Asia at the end of the nineteenth century. Like so many plants that do well in American temperate climates, loropetalums are native to China as well as to a single location in Japan. The Japanese, well-known for horticultural exuberance, have been largely responsible for the meteoric rise of this particular star.

Loropetalum is an easy plant to grow, thriving either in full sun or part shade. It is drought-tolerant, which is always good news, and is usable as a single specimen, in a mixed border, or as an informal hedge. "Informal" refers to loropetalum's loose growth habit. No amount of trimming will make loropetalum attractive as a formal sheared hedge, which I assume was the misbegotten goal of that parking lot marauder.

In my garden, I have two burgundy loropetalums in my mixed border and a single specimen loropetalum in the front border. A friend with a stone wall dropping to a busy street planted a loose hedge of green loropetalums along the top of the wall. She is encouraging branches to curve over the wall, giving her added privacy and softening the appearance of the gray stone.

Another friend with a bermed rock garden planted a dynamite combination of burgundy loropetalum, yellow barberry, and chartreuse conifers. Other ways to use this versatile and obliging shrub are espaliered against a wall or planted in a large container.

Loropetalums are vigorous but versatile growers, so buyer beware. Read the label carefully and make sure your choice will not outgrow its space. The species can grow up to twenty-five feet tall. However, most cultivars grow three to eight feet and dwarf varieties, such as *L. chinense* 'Ruby,' are being introduced for small gardens, mixed borders, and containers.

Last year I was among 400 gardeners who gasped aloud as we watched a horticulturist limb up a loropetalum into a tree shape to demonstrate the shrub's versatility. This is quite different from shearing one into a box or a sphere.

Loropetalum, like many multibranched shrubs, can be shaped into an attractive small tree when limited to three or five upright trunks with lower branches removed. The top is allowed to branch outward into a graceful sweep. Sort of a poor man's Japanese maple.

Along with many of those 400 astounded onlookers, I rushed home to clip a loropetalum in the mixed border into a small tree. This surgery added height to the border and gave me more room to plant ferns, perennials, and bulbs beneath it. I check it weekly to rub off new side shoots along the trunks, forbidding it to return to shrub form.

The leaves of loropetalum are small, overlapping, and heart-shaped. In my Southern garden, loropetalum is evergreen (actually ever-burgundy) but the foliage can be seared by heavy frost.

In fact, the shrub may be zapped to the ground by near-zero temperatures but will probably regenerate shoots as weather improves. Some new varieties are reported to be hardy at ten below zero.

The flowers, like witch hazel blooms, are spidery. The species has white flowers but flowers of cultivars such as 'Zhuzhou Fuchsia,' 'Fire Dance,' 'Blush,' and 'Ming Dynasty' are bright pink to almost red. Loropetalums bloom heavily in the spring and lightly through summer and fall.

Although all loropetalums have arching branches, growth habit varies. Again, read the label and do some research before plunking down your money (and your heart) for a plant that will outgrow its space or does not shape up as you wish it to. For example, 'Sizzlin Pink' has a horizontal growth habit while 'Pipa's Red' and 'Daybreak's Flame' are more layered.

As I write this, there are probably thirty loropetalum cultivars. By next year, there may very well be forty or more. You should be able to find the precise size, color, and shape you want in your garden. We saw this expansion in the nursery trade with crepe myrtles, and horticulturists are working diligently to supply the loropetalum demand, whatever it is.

Remember: As with crepe myrtles, the rule is to trim gently. Do not attempt to drastically reduce the size of your shrub or try to shape it into a structure it was never intended to become. You will work less, which is always happy news, and your loropetalum will live the good life in unfettered form.

Love Those Loropetalums

Lighten Up the Shade

For some reason, column ideas frequently pop into mind between my car and the church entrance. Almost every Sunday, going in or coming out, someone mentions his garden and I think, "Aha, there's a column in this question."

Just recently, as I hustled to get in the door without becoming part of the processional, another latecomer told me her garden was limited because of shade. My mind filled with shade plants, in spite of an effort to think spiritually rather than horticulturally.

Several years ago, after filling the sunny border across the back of our suburban yard, I did what all foolhardy gardeners do: I looked around for more planting space.

I had just read an article about planting an "island" and longed for one of my own. In front of the sunny border is a handsome old hickory tree. Beneath this tree lay untapped territory, in full view from my kitchen window but hampered by tree roots, falling nuts, and deep summer shade.

I marked out an oval island, leaving space at each end for pathways wide enough to push a wheelbarrow back to the border behind the island. Of course, over time this oval enlarged and, at present, only one pathway remains wide enough for a wheelbarrow.

I filled the island with a truckload of compost and was energized by the gorgeous blank soil canvas. It was so full of potential planting opportunities, so free of other plants to work around (except, of course, the hickory tree).

The compost was dumped on top of the lawn, already covered by thick layers of newspaper. Deprived of light, the grass gave up the ghost and so did weed seeds lying around waiting to germinate.

I never tilled this area. I also never dug up the grass that had struggled for life in the shade of the hickory tree. In fact, ever since I caught on to this strategy of covering grass (or weeds) with newspaper, compost, and mulch, I have never again dug up a bed or removed turf. Nature does the job effortlessly.

I planned my new island, keeping in mind that it would be shady in late spring, summer, and early fall. The shade would be dappled in early spring and late fall and heavy in summer, but the island would be in full sun during the winter months.

Shade-loving plants are actually more shade-tolerant than shade-amorous. Plants require light to do their chlorophyll thing. I remember that much from high school biology. I have discovered that many plants considered "full-sun" candidates appreciate shade, especially on mid-August afternoons.

I knew that proper island design requires that the tallest plants be placed in the center or spine of the island. All sides should be planted to present an attractive arrangement of midsize to low growing specimens. In other words, on an island there is no "behind" since all sides are on view.

Always the frugal gardener, I looked around my yard for shade-tolerant plants I could move or propagate. I read articles on shade gardening and looked for lists of shade-tolerant specimens. I looked at other gardens to see what thrived in locations similar to mine.

If this sounds like an organized scheme, do not be misled. I filled my space quickly with whatever was accessible or cheap, and many of the plants that started in the island wound up in other places or on a brush pile.

Few plants in this island or anywhere in my garden have not been moved at least once, and many have been moved multiple times. Most plants respond favorably to transportation, taking it as a sign the gardener cares about their comfort. Don't we all perk up when cherished?

Along the central spine of the island I planted summersweet (*Clethra alnifolia*); Virginia sweetspire (*Itea virginica* 'Henry Garnet'); fatsia; several hydrangeas; and devil's walking stick (*Aralia spinosa*), a long-limbed and thorny shrub with variegated leaves that light up the shade.

The most successful of the hydrangeas is *H. arborescens* 'Annabelle,' which loads herself up with fat white blooms in late spring and early summer. If I had room, I would add a variegated hydrangea. The blooms are insignificant but the foliage is spectacular in a healthy specimen.

I could also have planted aucuba, daphne, leucothoe, *Pieris japonica*, mahonia, leatherleaf viburnum, palms, or mid-sized camellias in this space. Perhaps I need another island.

I never considered hybrid azaleas since the South, where I garden, has a sufficiency. If space became available, however, I would be tempted to fill it with one of the native deciduous azaleas that, unlike their hybrid cousins, bloom in summer and are often scented.

Too many shaded gardens are green and nothing but. I am partial to green myself and enjoy someone else's foliage garden devoted to varied leaf-sizes and textures. But my shady garden blooms most of the year, beginning with winter daphnes and hellebores and ending in the fall with Japanese anemones.

In fact, many of my favorite bloomers show off in shade: the anemones, columbine, bright yellow woods poppies (*Stylophorum diphyllum*), cyclamen, epimediums, and Chinese mint shrub (*Elsholtzia stauntonii*).

Did I mention the no-longer functional clothesline that runs above this island? It is clothed in a Lady Banksia rose, which blooms before the tree leaves emerge, and sweet autumn clematis, which evidently does not care how deep the shade is.

Tucked here and there in this shady island are ferns, lady's mantle, acanthus, lemon verbena, rue, parsley, and a mass of groundcovers, including chameleon plant, lamium, creeping raspberry, sweet woodruff, golden creeping jennie, and white-flowered mazus.

My favorite groundcover is the barely half-inch-tall dwarf pennyroyal spreading outward and becoming an herbal lawn. More power to it, I say. We just mow right over it and let it grow.

To gardeners with "too much shade," count your blessings. Full-sun gardeners might happily trade.

Splendor in the Grasses

"Be still, my heart," I gasped as I went around the bend literally and figuratively at a nearby botanical garden last fall. There, next to the entrance, flowing over a corner, was a massive cloud of pink mist. *Muhlenbergia capillaris:* 'native sweet grass or hairy awn muhly' the label said. "Heaven," I sighed to myself. "Gotta have some."

As if I did not have sufficient horticultural passions to fill a lifetime, let alone a garden, it was love at first sight. I fell not just for *M. capillaris* but for ornamental grasses in general, and what a happy relationship it has turned out to be.

The attractions of ornamental grasses are many. Foremost, of course, is that they are beautiful plants, textured and fluid, always ready to move in the breeze, and tactile, inviting hands to move in and touch. Their colors are subtle unless they are burgundy like knee-high Japanese blood grass (*Imperata cylindrica* 'Red Baron') or purple-leaf sugarcane (*Saccharum officinarum* 'Pele's Smoke') that will reach eight to twelve feet in height. That is a lot of red.

But most ornamental grasses are varying shades of green, and I am grateful. Unlike lawn grass, which is green, green, green, ornamental grasses wear a rainbow of greens from chartreuse to kelly to almost-blue. They blend effectively in a mixed border and their varied textures soften the effect. I love color, and by midsummer my garden used to lean to flamboyance if not downright tackiness. I have learned to intersperse grasses to calm the garden down, giving the senses time to rest.

I like the tallest grasses such as eight- to ten-foot-high giant striped reed (*Arundo donax* 'Variegata') in the back of the border so the background hedge does not look like a dark green impenetrable wall. Midsized grasses go here and there in the middle of the garden, especially comfortable among prairie perennials such as coreopsis, black-eyed susans, and sunflowers. Short grasses edge areas of the border or serve as punctuation marks among groundcovers.

Ornamental grasses are variegated in the most extraordinary ways. In my garden I have several variegated *Miscanthus sinensis* plants: 'Cabaret' has a broad white band down the center of the leaf, 'Cosmopolitan' shows its white down either side of the leaf, and 'Strictus' and 'Zebrinus' wear their yellow stripes horizontally.

Early spring and fall are both good times to plant grasses. I like to buy a well-developed plant (on sale) and divide it into two or three sections. Grasses are not heavy feeders but they do best in soils rich in organic material. Too much nitrogen weakens them, and the foliage flops. Until the plants are established, keep the soil moist.

Grasses grow quickly, often reaching maximum height their first year. No waiting around for three years as we do with most perennials before they reach lush maturity. They are easy to grow and maintain, unbothered for the most part by insects and diseases.

Many ornamental grasses, such as switch grass (*Panicum virgatum*), Indian grass (*Sorghastrum*), bluestem (*Andropogon*), and cord grass (*Spartina*), are prairie grasses, acclimated to heat, wind, drought, and cold, cold winters. I have never seen an ornamental grass in a garden expire because of climate. Or any other reason, now that I think of it.

Most grasses, in fact, are at their best during those merciless days of summer when everything else is in a funk. Eulalia grass (*Miscanthus sinensis*), feather reed grass (*Calamagrostis acutiflora* Stricta), and fountain grass (*Pennisetum alopecuroides*) are perkiest when the gardener is sweatiest.

Grasses in general enjoy sun but a number of them tolerate shade. I am especially fond of gold and green *Carex elata* 'Bowles Golden' and variegated *C. phyllocephala* 'Sparkler,' which grow successfully in part sun or shade. More than most grasses, carex, not technically a grass but a grass lookalike, prefers moist conditions. *C. phyllocephala* 'Sparkler' is one of my all-time favorite plants in the garden. It has green and white variegated foliage that looks like little palm trees dancing to a tropical beat.

Except for Latin names that defy pronunciation and memory, ornamental grasses have only one major flaw. Most are hard to move once they settle in. Fortunately, they do not need dividing for five to ten years after planting. When the time comes, divide as new growth emerges in the spring. For the operation, you will need a shovel as well as an axe, preferably in the hands of a strong man. Of course, you can refuse to divide grasses at all without fear of arrest.

In early spring, with manual or electric hedge clippers, cut grasses down to three or four inches to tidy them up and stimulate new growth. Some tall grasses (miscanthus, especially) reportedly benefit from a repeat cutting around the Fourth of July to keep them from flopping over. I have never done this myself but understand they recover quickly and regain their full height in several weeks.

Deadheading is tough on a gardener's tender heart because grass seeds are so attractive on the plants. However, some grasses (including miscanthus and pennisetum) seed heavily and may become invasive. I cut the stems off and bring them indoors for winter arrangements, though I would much rather leave them for the birds.

Shrubbing It Up

The older I get, the more attracted I am to shrubs. Especially flower-ing and berrying shrubs that change with the seasons and add pizzazz to a mixed border.

I choose to believe this attraction stems from horticultural sophis-tication rather than aging joints, though I admit to regarding shrubs as a kind of insurance. I know that, no matter how decrepit I become, well-chosen shrubs can provide a garden of surprise and joy for every season with minimum effort on my part.

Fall is the best time to think about shrubs and to plant them since rain is usually plentiful. The soil is pleasant to work and digging holes is not too laborious, especially if someone else does them for you. Young shrubs have all winter to develop roots and will be prepared to withstand the onslaught of heat and drought next summer.

When you are cruising nurseries and plant sales for shrubs to add to your collection, make sure they are not rootbound by tipping them out of the pots to take a look. However, if you discover the plant of your dreams at a good price and it proves to be rootbound, before planting, shake or cut the roots loose before placing it in the hole. I take a sharp knife and make a swipe from top to bottom in several places along the sides and also loosen or trim off the compacted bot-tom roots.

When planting a shrub or almost any other plant, I dig the hole no deeper than the plant sits in the pot and two to three times the di-ameter of the pot. If I gardened in clay or heavy loam, I would loosen the soil at the bottom of the hole to encourage root development downward as well as outward. In my sandy loam, roots head down-ward without hesitation.

I used to add compost when planting, but the soil in my borders, after years of mulching with hay, is as humusy as a compost pile. Sometimes I mix in a handful of pelleted dolomitic lime but I do not add fertilizer to the soil. If the soil lacks nutrients, I scatter slow-release fertilizer or organic amendments *on top of the soil* before adding a mulch of hay, shredded leaves, pine bark, or pinestraw. Finally I water the plant site to settle the roots.

This is a dramatic change from what we used to think was necessary to plant a shrub. We dug deep holes and incorporated all kinds of amendments and then put the shrub in just a bit deeper than it sat in the pot as extra protection. The last thing we did was stomp around the shrub to settle the soil and get rid of air pockets.

As with many good deeds, intentions were honorable but outcomes were often disappointing. Roots tended to stay put or remain in a circular pattern rather than wander outward seeking nourishment and moisture. Because shrubs were planted too deeply, we literally suffocated the top layer of roots that are the most active in seeking nutrients. And our dance around the shrub did further injury to feeder roots.

It is a wonder such ill-treated plants survived at all, though we know they did and have hale and hearty mature shrubs as proof. The point is, however, that we do not have to work nearly as hard as we thought and our shrubs will thrive. Now isn't that a bit of good news?

If you are as serious as I am about creating a garden of shrubs, select them with the same attention to color, texture, shape, and size as you would with perennials and other plants. A shrub border is not a row of hollies, camellias, conifers, or anything else. It is a mixture of plants that provides four seasons of interest, a tapestry of green, burgundy, gold, and variegated foliage, fragrance, and a rich variety of textures.

My favorite shrubs have two or even three seasons of interest, but some shrubs, such as deciduous hollies, covered all winter with bright red or orange berries, can be forgiven if they do not offer much the other three seasons.

I like to see a variety of forms in a shrub border: rounded, creeping, pyramidal, but no squares or balls. Appreciate plants in their natural forms. Remember, although a shrub border should be a scene of beauty, one of its main purposes is to relieve you of labor.

Consider natural structure and mature sizes. Read the labels and search out new dwarf cultivars of almost every shrub species. Shop diligently and you just may be able to toss your hedge clippers away. Now that is really good news!

No matter where you are in your gardening life, approaching dotage or just starting out, a shrub border can become a glorious garden within a few years, providing fragrance, flowers to cut, berries, nesting area for the birds, and richly colored foliage. What more does a gardener want . . . other than more time to sit and admire?

A Kick out of Cleaning Up

Cleaning house has never been an even tolerable pastime as far as I am concerned. I can think of no more boring tasks than dusting and scrubbing. But tidying up the garden at the end of the growing season is not only fun; it is also a challenge, a treasure hunt, and a new beginning.

I am one of those gardeners for whom the growing season never ends. I can find something interesting in my garden from January 1 through December 31, and this is a good thing. Checking out the garden in the morning gets me going, and I am afraid that if the garden had nothing to admire each day, I might not get going at all.

On cool sunny days, I crawl around on my hands and knees, looking for treasure: plump little offshoots to be dug and potted up. I ease them out of the soil with my fingers and a knife, making sure that each offshoot has a set of independent roots.

If an offshoot is fairly good size and well rooted, I may plant it in another location. Usually I pot up promising offshoots in quart-size containers filled with two-thirds potting mix and one-third rich garden soil or compost. Then I put the pots in a protected area where they will get morning sun and I will remember to water them if we hit a dry spell.

Do not baby the plants. You would be surprised by the number of people who want to keep them inside. These plants are perennials, which means they either never die back or they go into dormancy and reappear in spring. In other words, these plants endure and perhaps even enjoy winter.

If you are a real softie, you can pamper potted perennials just a bit by burying them in mulch or sinking them into soil, but such coddling should not be necessary. I do not do it myself but I am not a coddler by nature, as my children will attest.

I divide spring-blooming perennials that are overgrown or have lost vigor. I dig them up, taking advantage of that empty hole to add a few shovels of compost. I do not add any other soil amendment. If I want to fertilize (which I rarely do), I wait until early spring rather than risk stimulating foliage. I want root growth now, not leaves.

I move misplaced plants to other sites where I hope they will be happier. Few plants in my garden are in their original locations, and some have been moved twice or more.

I lack design sense, other than knowing that tall plants usually should be toward the back and short ones in the front. It is only after I have lived with plant combinations awhile that I realize I can do better. Fortunately, plants are not hard to move until they get large, and by then I have generally, but not always, made up my mind.

I plant newly purchased shrubs, trees, and perennials in fall so they can spend the winter growing roots that should enable them to survive the following summer. If I wait until spring to do my planting, the roots will soon be stressed by summer drought and heat. If they are planted in the fall, they spend winter and spring expanding roots into cool damp soil, turning into tough survivors by the time 100-degree days arrive.

Be sure to gather seeds of annuals such as melampodium, zinnias, globe amaranth, cypress vine, Mexican sunflowers, and other nonhybridized favorites. Saving seeds is a satisfying task, giving you a smug sense of facilitating the natural life cycle.

In the spring, you can recycle these seeds by planting them in your garden or sharing with other gardeners. Some of my favorite plants have come from seeds given to me by friends or from seedpods borrowed from gardens I visit.

Find mulch where you can—cheap is good, free is ideal—and spread it over your garden. Pinestraw, leaves, well-shredded bark, or hay will do fine. While I mulch new beds with six to eight inches on top of newspaper, I mulch established borders with just three or four inches. In a short time, the organic material packs down and eventually becomes part of the soil, which is why I rarely fertilize.

If you are lucky, you can find spoiled hay, unusable as feed because it has gotten wet and moldy. But even if you have to spend real dollars on enough bales to blanket your garden, it is an excellent investment.

And, finally, we come to the hard part of garden cleanup, especially if you think neatness comes anywhere close to godliness. Garner your self-discipline. If necessary, ask your spouse or sympathetic neighbor to hide hedge clippers, pruners, and loppers. You must restrain yourself from leveling every fading plant.

Leave all stalks and stems, seedheads, and dried grasses to provide cover and perches as well as food for birds and other wildlife. Beneficial insects, lizards, and toads require cover to survive the winter. Butterfly chrysalises need stems and branches to hang on. Garden disorder seems a small price to pay when we are talking about sustaining life for significant creatures.

You will also be providing "winter interest" for yourself and other garden-savvy folk. Now I know that dried stalks and stems can hardly compare to a flourishing garden, but surely they are less offensive than Absolutely Nothing to Look At.

Admittedly, winter interest is in the eye of the beholder, especially the beholder who has trained herself to see natural phenomena as not only fascinating but also reassuring. The creatures we shelter benefit our environment. Stalks and grasses enrich our soil, and the discoveries we make enhance our lives.

A Kick out of Cleaning Up

CHAPTER 3

Winter

Winter is a time for standing back, assessing the bones,
and pondering the future.

Leave the Leaves

Just before Christmas, I was chatting with friends about our gardens in the winter when one of them asked what I do about "all those leaves."

I was astonished to hear her admit to hand picking hers from the border and depositing them in a bucket. I hadn't the heart to ask what she did with the bucketful of discarded leaves, hoping she had at least put them in a leaf pile for composting. I suspect they were placed in plastic bags and left at the curb for pick-up, as if they were full of trash instead of riches.

Leaves, as well as garden clippings and kitchen scraps, are the makings of humus, that natural resource we pay exorbitant prices for when it comes from the garden center. We buy truckloads of all kinds of compost but discard the very stuff that turns into compost if we leave it alone. I just do not get it.

Now I too buy compost by the truckload as well as by the bag because I never have enough. But I also create my own by piling up debris, mulching with shredded leaves and hay, and tucking kitchen waste (vegetable peels, rinds, eggshells, coffee grounds, anything but meat and grease) under the mulch. Except for a rotating barrel that I roll on occasion, I have no compost pile but, instead, I have compost pile-ettes all over the yard. Unless I lift the mulch to show them off or a neighbor's dog decides they are of passing interest, garden visitors are unaware of my continual compost manufacturing.

I keep a bucket under the sink and deposit kitchen debris until the bucket is full. Then I trot out to the garden, pick a spot, empty the bucket, cover with mulch, and stomp around a little on top to hasten the composting process. The bucket goes back to the kitchen and I start again. In a couple of days, I have another bucketful of compost makings to take to the garden.

The mixture of kitchen waste and leaves is manna from heaven to beneficial fungi, insects, worms, bacteria, and microscopic invertebrates that add air and nutrients to the soil.

But back to those leaves in the border that bother my tidy friend enough so she crawls around on hands and knees, lifting them out for disposal. I shudder to think of all that work when she could be reading a book or lying in a hammock.

I also ponder the irony that, while I am putting leaves *on* my borders, she is taking them *off* hers.

In winter, my garden looks as straggly and beige as everyone else's, stragglier probably since I do not cut down dead stems or remove the last spent blooms. From December on, everything remains pretty much as is. In late February or early March, I prune buddleias and other summer shrubs.

The clean-up urge hits as daffodils emerge, which, in my garden, begins in late February. That is when I do my own crawling around, primarily to see what is coming up and to discover plants I had forgotten or misplaced. This is not work. It is fun and full of surprises, which is precisely what gardening should be.

Everything is protected by a blanket of leaves and uncut stems, just as nature intended. As buds begin swelling toward winter's end, I clip off spent blooms and dried stems, cut ornamental grasses to the ground, and prune the hedge and foundation plants. I remove dead branches (those without buds) from hydrangeas and cut those that bloom on *new* wood to the ground. If you are not sure when your hydrangeas bloom, leave them alone until you figure it out. Other shrubs that bloom in the spring (such as azaleas, mock orange, and weigela) should be left unpruned until after they flower.

My advice to my friend who wants her garden neat and unsullied by dead leaves is to look at what nature does and do the same. Leave leaves where they fall (within reason) and add some more. Think of bare branches, dried grass, and seedheads as "winter interest" that cutting-edge garden designers admire.

Why is bare earth more attractive than a blanket of crisp leaves or rich brown mulch? Why are trimmed branches more desirable than dried hydrangea blooms that turn a warm beige or, better yet, purple? Why remove seedheads that attract birds? Or trim foliage that provides shelter?

Perhaps we should regard garden neatness less as a virtue and more as a waste. Focus with the garden designers on winter interest instead of the mess. And just think of all the books we can read and naps we can take, not to mention the good deeds we can do, in the time it takes to do the cleanup.

Leave the Leaves

Some Gifts Cannot Be Wrapped

I wish I felt sure that the adage, "With age comes wisdom," was true. I do know that as I have added years I have learned that, when the gift is right, it is more fun to give than to receive. I also discovered that I need not possess an item to treasure it, and that it really is the thought that counts.

A dear friend of mine gave a gift to her garden: a name. I can see why. A garden is such an integral part of our lives and our spirits, it becomes a friend as well as a refuge. A friend should be called by name.

My friend and her husband took a trip to Poland and, while there, she visited a small Jewish cemetery called "Beracha." A Polish friend translated for her: "Beracha is a blessing . . . a divine goodness flowing into the world." And that is the name my friend has given to her garden. A gift to the garden that is, in turn, a gift to all who visit it.

The sign on my garden says "Rejoice," but that is more an order or request than a name. Perhaps I should call it "Joy."

In the spirit of gift giving, I started thinking of other treats to give a garden. The same friend who owns Beracha revives her garden every year, plot by plot, by pulling everything out, digging out the top twelve inches of soil, and loosening up the twelve inches of soil below. After putting back the top twelve inches she amends it with alfalfa pellets, chicken manure, cottonseed meal, lime, and peat moss. She then replants.

Her soil is luscious and I am in awe. Her garden is appreciative, as you can imagine, and every plant thrives. If you ask me, she is the beracha and her garden knows it.

I, on the other hand, take a more leisurely path to garden fulfillment. I give my garden lots of appreciation, a great deal of mulch, and occasional amendments on no particular schedule.

Another friend gathered up her husband and two friends and gave someone else's garden what I consider the ultimate gift: a day of weeding, digging, planting, and the tender loving care that gardeners give the earth. And it was a surprise! The recipient had just moved out of an abusive marriage into a new home and, while she was at work, the Garden Fairies showed up with rakes and shovels.

They had such a good time, my friend told me, that they have decided to do four projects a year. No organization, no dues, just a loose-knit group of friends who have many blessings in their own lives and the grace to share with others.

My sign, the one that reminds me to rejoice, hangs on an arbor built for me by one of my sons a few Christmases ago. He precut the lumber, brought it to our house, and, on Christmas day, he, his brother, and their dad put the arbor together. This was a perfect gift, one enjoyed every day of my life and a continual reminder of how fortunate I am.

For Christmas, birthdays, weddings, births, and other celebrations, no gift lasts longer than a tree or serves as such a continual reminder of love. A tree is also a lasting memorial, reminding us of our loss but evoking thoughts of good times and vitality.

The plants I treasure most in my own garden came from the gardens of friends as casual gifts. Among my favorite words are "Would you like a cutting? Or a seedling? Or some seeds?" These too are gifts that remind us continually of the giver. I guess diamond earrings might have the same effect, but I prefer gifts that grow.

If an organization or institution has blessed you or someone you love with faith, learning, or happiness, why not give a donation of a tree or a shrub or a garden in gratitude. I occasionally plant and tend a small garden at our county's arts center and take pleasure in knowing that people who support the arts in our community enjoy it. If only they would deadhead from time to time. They know who they are.

The gifts of time and attention may be the most treasured of all. Take a friend to a botanical garden or arboretum, especially a friend who might be unable to get there on her own. No matter what month of the year, there is something to see and admire. Have someone take your picture together perhaps, as a souvenir for your guest. Share a picnic or go somewhere swell for lunch.

Please do not leave the birds off your gift list. Trim a tree with bird delights such as strings of berries, suet balls, nuts, pinecones smeared with peanut butter, and other goodies. Be sure to provide water for your guests to drink and to bathe in. Give them a heater or dripper for the birdbath to keep the water from freezing, and add a birdhouse or two for shelter and nesting.

And to yourself, give a pat on the back for the care you give this earth, for sharing with others, and for finding happiness in simply growing good things.

Divide and Expand

Call me sentimental, but I love Christmas. I wallow in good cheer. I never tire of Christmas carols, exchanging gifts, or consuming a shocking number of calories. I like to hear strangers wish one another "Merry Christmas," and I feel good when I see a pile of gifts for children who would have no Christmas if it were not for the generosity of anonymous people.

But, like most people, I tire of the commercialism that saturates the season. I feel guilty about having too much food and too much stuff. As usual, when I am frustrated or grumpier than usual, I head for my garden where serenity reigns and, even in December, there are pleasant tasks to do.

An autumn fern (*Dryopteris erythrosora*) I purchased at an end-of-season sale needs repotting. I work the overgrown fern out of its pot, take a sharp knife, and cut the plant into four vertical sections, producing four autumn ferns for the price of one. With the same knife, I slit the sides of each section, slicing through roots, and then I cut off the bottom two inches of roots that are a solid mass. I massage the remaining root mass to loosen it up.

Sometimes when I do this surgery, I stick the plant slices directly in the garden, adding a little compost and plenty of moisture. This works best if you are planting in the shade and you are able to keep the soil damp for the next couple of weeks, not sopping wet (which might rot the roots) but comfortably moist.

If the divided plant is going into a sunny location, especially when the days are hot, I usually pot up the divisions in compost-enriched potting mix and keep them in a shady spot until the weather cools or until I decide where I want them. Sometimes I pot up a couple and plant a couple.

Garden centers have terrific sales as one season ends and another begins. Most of them do not have the labor force to repot plants that outgrow their containers, so they pass them along at bargain prices to customers who are willing to take the five minutes or so that it takes to tip out, slice, and repot.

Sometimes, of course, you cannot divide (but you can almost always conquer). For instance, a single-trunk shrub is not to be sliced into sections, no matter how rootbound it is. Before planting it, however, with your trusty sharp knife, slice the sides of the rootball vertically, remove badly matted roots at the bottom, and shake or tease the roots to loosen them. You want the roots to grow outward, not around and around as if they were still in a container.

I have heard people shudder as they watch this operation but, believe me, it does not hurt. Your plant will feel better with loose roots and, even if it is set back by the drastic surgery, it will recover with a little tender loving care from you.

If you have run out of space in your garden plots, it is time to expand. December is an ideal time to get started, but so is any other time of the year. Whether you are adding to an old border or starting a new one, mark the area where you want your new garden space. If you want the border to curve, use a hose or rope or spray paint to mark the boundaries. If you prefer straight lines, use a few pointed sticks and some string to mark the perimeter.

DO NOT REMOVE THE GRASS unless you need it somewhere else. Do not dig and do not even think about tilling. Place newspaper, about eight sheets thick, over the entire area. Make sure edges overlap to keep out light. Cover the newspapers with four inches of compost and cover the compost with mulch of hay, pinestraw, shredded leaves, or shredded pine bark.

You now have a sandwich of eight sheets of newspaper, four or more inches of compost, and six to eight inches of mulch. Go inside and read seed catalogs or wrap a few presents.

What a gift you have given yourself: a blank canvas to create your next garden masterpiece. You have the rest of winter to make plans. By March, the area will be flattened considerably. You may have to cut through the newspaper to plant but, like all good mulch, in time it will become part of your soil. So will the grass.

Another gift to yourself is a notebook or journal or calendar in which to write notes about your plans and observations. I have friends who keep copious notes in journals about the progress of their gardens. They take photographs and tape in pertinent clippings from magazines.

I admire these friends and try to emulate them. I love to read a garden journal, especially my own, though it is sporadic and unillustrated. But for day-to-day reminders of what to put where, when to transplant, and whom to ask for cuttings, nothing works as well for me as a calendar with a whole month on a single page and ample space for jotting notes.

How fortunate we are to have our garden getaways where there is always something pleasant to do, some task that makes us look toward the future. Away from the malls and out in the garden, we fill our borders with plants and our lives with good cheer.

Divide and Expand

A Twisted Tale of Vines

I have an acquaintance with an enormous house surrounded by acres of property. The entire perimeter of the property is marked by a handsome fence.

The house is old and well kept, a historical landmark and architecturally beautiful, the kind of place regularly featured on tours of grand homes in antebellum towns.

It is not the house I desire, however. I tend to think of the housekeeping involved when visiting large and elaborately decorated residences, and I know they are not for me.

Even the property around this particular house does not tempt me. It too would require at least two overworked groundskeepers to keep the landscaping in tiptop condition.

It is the fence I covet. I long for half a mile or so of fence on which I could drape vines. I could never limit myself to one or even multiples of two; I would plant at least a dozen different perennial vines and then overplant them with annuals. My fence would be a thing of beauty all year long and, from time to time, would burst forth with surprises of color and scent.

The first vine to go on the fence would be confederate jasmine (*Trachelospermum jasminoides*), which grows in both sun and shade so I could plant it at intervals for continuity. This vine is an enthusiastic grower but easily restrained with occasional pruning to keep the foliage thick and luxuriant. It blooms best, of course, with plenty of sunlight and actually prefers hot weather, most definitely a Southerner. The blooms are small and white and the scent is heavenly.

I would grow Carolina yellow jessamine (*Gelsemium sempervirens*) in the sunniest area of my fence. I like the glossy small leaves, the unassuming yellow blooms, and the fact that it blooms at the first hint of spring.

I would also plant five-leaf akebia (*Akebia quinata*), which has small maroon flowers, not too exciting except for their subtle fragrance. What I admire is the lacy-looking gray-green trifoliate leaves of this enthusiastic grower. It tends to wander afar but stray stems pull up easily.

Sweet autumn clematis (*Clematis paniculata*) would look wonderful on my fence, adding texture with its foliage, fragrant white flowers, and, at the end of the season, a mass of fluffy seedpods. Someone told me recently that this vine attracts mosquitoes, but I do not believe it. Another friend complains about it "coming up everywhere," but I have not found this a problem either, perhaps because I mulch thickly and also because I do not mind bending over and pulling up a few wayward plants. A small price to pay for such a super show.

In a sunny location, I would plant Lady Banksia rose (*Rosa banksia*) to greet the spring with a bower of little yellow (or white) roses that look delicate but are not. I would cut her back severely after she blooms to encourage new growth and an abundance of blooms the following year.

In my fenceless garden, Lady Banksia drapes herself like a strumpet across half of an unused clothesline. I also encourage her to grow up a pine tree. When one does not have a fence to call her own, a gardener has to be resourceful.

On the fence I envision, I would plant summer-blooming Madame Galen trumpet creeper (*Campsis xtagliabuana* 'Madame Galen') with lush wisteria-like foliage, exotic orange blooms, and long bean-like seedpods. Hummingbirds love this flamboyant lady.

Common honeysuckle (*Lonicera japonica*) would be planted near my work area so I could treat myself to a whiff of haunting scent when I do my potting up. The native orange and yellow trumpet honeysuckle (*Lonicera sempervirens*) would be displayed more prominently. Though it lacks scent, it packs a visual wallop and attracts hummingbirds and butterflies, honored guests in my garden.

I could not say no to wisteria. After all, I have half a mile of fence to cover, so I would plant both Japanese wisteria, the most fragrant as well as the most rampant, and Chinese wisteria, which blooms later.

The native selection, *Wisteria frutescens* 'Amethyst Falls,' would have pride of place on my fence for good reason. It blooms after the Asians and, get this, blooms again in mid- and late summer. Did I mention that the blooms are blue?

In an area that has partial shade I would plant climbing hydrangea (*Hydrangea anomala petiolaris*), which is slow to get started but spectacular once it gets going, with large clusters of white flowers just as you would expect on a plant called hydrangea.

But I might not be able to wait years for those flowers, so I would grow *Schizophragma hydrangeoides* 'Moonlight,' a hydrangea look-alike with silver-frosted foliage and flowers that deserve the romantic name.

A vine that can be a nuisance, passionflower (*Passiflora xcaerulea*), would go on my fence as well. The flowers are incredibly exotic and complex. This is a vine that will show up in surprising places, but, like sweet autumn clematis, it is easy to pull up and keeps the gardener flexible and on her toes.

The native orange flowered cross vine (*Bignonia radicans*) would go somewhere on my fence and so would golden hops (*Humulus lupulus* 'Aureus'). The joy of having so much fence is that I can have so many vines, but picking and choosing are still not easy.

Annual vines, which I would grow up and around and over the perennials, would include sweet potato vines (*Ipomoea batatas,* both chartreuse and deep purple). I know they usually trail along the ground but, as I recently discovered, they will also climb a tree or trellis. I would plant exotic love or firecracker vine (*Mina lobata*), which bursts into bloom in late summer after lolling around for months; and cypress vine (*Ipomoea quamoclit*) with little red tubular blooms to lure butterflies and hummingbirds.

And then there are hyacinth bean, moon vine, black-eyed susan vine, and asarina. The list goes on, but isn't that the way gardening is supposed to happen? Our gardens are works in progress and so are the gardeners.

Sometimes the News Is Good

I was heartened by this story reported by Anne Raver, garden columnist for the *New York Times*. Weeks after the 9/11 catastrophe, a thousand houseplants were delivered to Stuyvesant High School just a few blocks from Ground Zero.

Not surprisingly, high levels of airborne particles had been found in the building by an environmental engineer hired by the school's parents organization. A Stuyvesant biology teacher was aware of the work of Dr. William Wolverton, an environmental scientist with NASA, who in the 1980s had measured the amazing abilities of common houseplants to remove chemicals from the air.

According to Raver, the principal called wholesale nurseryman, Eric Keil, to order a houseplant for each classroom, 150 in all. Knowing that one plant was not going to be effective, Keil did some networking, and 1,000 palms, peace lilies, and philodendrons (top air cleaners according to the Wolverton study) were donated by twenty members of the Florida Nursery and Growers Association.

Chet Peckett, a wholesale grower in Florida, had arranged for the shipment of donated plants worth $15,000. The shipping company did not charge for delivery. The plants arrived on Election Day when school was closed, so local volunteers showed up to unload the truck and deliver plants to each classroom.

"I don't know how much the plants can do—but it's got to help some," nurseryman Eric Keil told Raver.

Keil was right. Whether they cleared the air sufficiently or not, 1,000 lush green plants had to improve morale among Stuyvesant's students and faculty when they walked into school the next day and discovered that people they did not know cared about the air they breathed.

This is a story about people as much as it is about plants. Many ordinary people donated plants, time, energy, and resources to make a difference at Stuyvesant High School. As I recall my own overwhelming feelings of helplessness and anger after 9/11, I regard this story as a moving example of American generosity and initiative when the going got tough.

Peckett offered to send more plants, if needed. "You could put air purifiers in," he told Raver, "but you won't get the emotional comfort of having live plants around."

Even in normal circumstances, most of us spend much of our lives in houses and workplaces where windows are shut year round. We have managed to increase fuel efficiency by caulking and insulation, but we have fouled the air we breathe with fumes from office machine chemicals, dyes, paint, plastics, and household cleaners. Just recently, I heard that our indoor spaces can be more polluted than metropolitan streets. That is scary.

But we can do something about these toxins by supplying our houses and workspaces with plants and letting nature take its course. Here is more good news: According to studies conducted by the National Space Technologies Lab, the most efficient air-cleaning plants do well in low-light sites, are among the least expensive, and are easy to care for.

No doubt about their effectiveness. An ordinary spider plant was placed in a sealed chamber filled with formaldehyde fumes that are emitted naturally by plastics and building materials. The toxic fumes were reduced by 85 percent in twenty-four hours.

This is what happens. The plants take in the chemicals with carbon dioxide through their leaves, break the chemicals down, and return clean oxygen. Furthermore, the roots and microbes in the potting mix also neutralize chemicals by consuming them as food.

Almost all plants do this without injury to themselves, but some plants are more effective than others. In addition to spider plants, peace lilies, palms, and philodendrons, other pollution-preventing plants are the old reliables our mothers and grandmothers used to grow: pothos, corn plants, Chinese evergreens, English ivy, rubber plants, schefflera, and mother-in-law's tongue.

Ironically, most gardeners I know are not fond of indoor plants. I have killed my own share of them by overwatering or general neglect. But I believe we have reached the point when houseplants may very well be lifesaving necessities and well worth the little bit of care they require and whatever they cost.

Look at the areas in your house where you spend blocks of time: bedrooms, the family room, office and hobby areas, the kitchen and dining table. Wherever you are, your breathing zone is six to eight cubic feet surrounding you. Groups of five or more plants in each frequently used area will add humidity and remove toxins from the air you and your family are breathing.

Here is a tip for those with asthma or allergies to mold and fungus. Cover the potting mix in each container with an inch or two of aquarium or pea gravel so the surface will stay dry. Be sure no water sits in the saucer under the pot. You might want to investigate growing houseplants hydroponically (in water) using a special fertilizer.

Dr. Wolverton, now retired from NASA and president of Wolverton Environmental Services, wonders why it took us so long to realize that plants could clean the air indoors, since we know we could not survive without plants to purify and revitalize the outdoor air.

I suspect the solution was overlooked because of its simplicity. Our faith in technology is so fervent and unquestioning that we underestimate the miracles Mother Nature performs as a matter of course, to our good fortune.

Sometimes the News Is Good

Them Bones, Them Bones

Next time we have one of those warm winter days that remind us that winter does not last forever, take time to step outside, breathe deeply, and think gardening thoughts. The oxygen you inhale will fill you with hope and enthusiasm, just the stuff gardeners use to energize themselves for spring.

Walk around and admire the winter features of your garden. Enjoy the sculptural shapes and textures. Take note of the variety of leaf forms and sizes. Observe the abundance of greens provided by nature even in early February. Notice the shadows. Look for the purples and grays that dress up the garden any time of the year, but are especially appreciated when flowers are scarce.

As you stroll, take inventory. Make notes about areas that need perking up, plants that should be moved, areas that need height or the addition of groundcover. At this time of the year, when annuals are gone and most perennials are reduced to twigs and stubble, you are looking at "the bones" of your garden.

My own garden is left during the winter pretty much as Mother Nature directs. I remove annuals, but I leave everything else until late winter, when the garden and I are ready to begin again. As a result, I know where everything (or almost everything) is and where the holes are. I have, I will admit, a heap of dead foliage hanging around, but I like to think of it as shelter for wildlife and mulch-in-the-making.

Two winter favorites in my Southern garden are fatsia and cast iron plant (*Aspidistra elatior*), which manage to look tropical even if the water in the birdbath is frozen solid. They are great shade plants but, like the gardener, they enjoy occasional sun.

The rich burgundy color of loropetalum is at its best, I think, among all the beiges, tans, and drab browns of the winter garden. I have two in the mixed border that runs across the back of our property and one in the front landscape. For even more purple, I plant winter-hardy Russian kale and giant red mustard where summer annuals were pulled out. They are mostly for looks, but we enjoy eating them on occasion and feel virtuous about ingesting all those vitamins.

Longing for yellow? Add variegated aucuba or euonymus. Both of these easy-to-grow evergreen shrubs are deep forest green splashed with yellow. They are mainstays in flower arrangements, but they can hold their own all by themselves in a vase as well as in the garden.

My all-time favorite foliage is blue-gray. It provides rich contrast to all the brighter colors in our gardens and a lush softness in the winter garden. Many perennial herbs are what I call "evergray," so remind yourself, when spring rolls around, to plant gray santolina, artemisias, lavender, wormwood, rue, lamb's ears, and rosemary to dress up your garden throughout the year.

Once you have enjoyed the winter interest in your own garden, the best places to discover plants that keep the garden interesting in our coldest months are other people's gardens. I love visiting gardens any time of the year, but I find it especially informative to do so when my own garden needs spiffing up.

If you are looking for gardening inspiration or just a midwinter treat, head for the nearest botanical garden or arboretum in your area. These gardens, open year round to the public, are absolute treasures when it comes to spreading the news of cutting-edge plants for the area in which you live.

Most every plant in well-tended botanical gardens is labeled. Furthermore, the gardens are usually staffed with knowledgeable gardeners, especially willing to chat during winter months when they are unstressed and perhaps even lonesome. They may get paid, but they are still gardeners who love sharing information and perhaps seeds and cuttings as well.

Do not forget to feed the birds and keep water available for them. In return, they will provide continuing entertainment and feel encouraged to stay in the neighborhood to gobble up troublesome insects in spring, which we all know is right around the corner.

Them Bones, Them Bones

Follies in the Foundation

We have done it again. The overgrown hollies and variegated pit-tosporum across the front of our house have been leveled by Chain Saw Man. Fortunately, the mayhem is partially hidden behind a row of low growing chartreuse spireas, so it will not look as bad from the street as it does from inside the house. I hope.

I read about garden design all the time. I clip pictures from garden magazines. I listen to lectures and have visited gardens created by some of the world's best designers. Yet I still find myself wandering around my yard, potted plant clutched to my bosom, just looking for a bit of space. This lack of system has worked well in the mixed borders in the back yard. I just pack plants in, attempting to vary foliage, to coordinate colors, and to consider proportions. The results are quite satisfying. Stunning, sometimes.

The front yard, however, is an embarrassment. Our house, built in the late sixties, is typical of the era: ranch style, long across the front, sturdy but no extraordinary architectural furbishes. Like everyone else on our street, we planted a row of green stuff across the front and along the sides and turned our attention to child raising.

The children grew and so did the green stuff, so we began cutting overgrown shrubs to the ground occasionally, letting them grow out, and, when inevitably they grew too tall, cutting them down again. In the meantime we went to ball games, had birthday parties, and attended PTO meetings.

Our three-foot-tall Helleri hollies (*Ilex crenata* 'Helleri'), the shrubs planted by everyone on our street and maybe everyone in our state, became leggy and unattractive in about ten years.

We cut them down and planted Dwarf Burford hollies (*Ilex cornuta* 'Burfordii Nana'). "Dwarf" is a relative term. A thirty-foot conifer can be a dwarf if the species conifer is sixty feet. Of course, the Burford hollies grew too tall and we have had to cut them down at least three times. For about a year after being cut, they are just right: several inches below the window line, full and fulsome with shiny green leaves and a crop of red berries for Christmas decorating. The following year, they head toward the eaves.

If we had used the brains that got us each a college education, we would have planted shorter shrubs in front of the original Helleri hollies to cover their legginess and distract from their general unattractiveness. While this would not have been inspired landscaping, it would have done the job and we never would have purchased the Burford hollies, nor would we have been cutting them to the ground every five years to control their height.

Some time ago, when I could no longer stand those boring Burford hollies marching alone across the front of the house, I did plant those chartreuse spireas (*Spirea xbumalda* 'Goldflame') in front of the hollies. This was another boring row of shrubs, but the foliage is chartreuse, which adds pizzazz. For good measure, I planted variegated liriope in front of the spirea. Black mondo grass would have been a more striking choice, but the liriope was free and tolerable.

In the corner by the front door, we planted variegated pittosporum. One plant looked ridiculous in the space, so we planted three, all of which have grown enormous so we cut them down to the ground too.

At the corners of the house are the same Burford hollies, which are now ten feet tall and have been trimmed into trees. I like the effect, though they are a nuisance to keep trimmed. The area next to the driveway was originally full of azaleas but I tired of them, too, so I have planted a mixture of shade-loving shrubs, providing something of interest all year long.

The area at the other end of the house, in full sun all day, is a work in progress and probably will remain so. I am leaning toward burgundy loropetalum or barberry, both of which come in appropriate sizes for this space, and more of the chartreuse spirea. When I like something, I tend to be excessive.

If I had it to do over again, I mean really do over and not just patch up, I would forget about rows of anything and plant the front the same way I planted the borders in the back yard. I would have no more than three of anything and most shrubs would be limited to one, just as they are in the mixed borders.

I would include deciduous shrubs as well as conifers. I would incorporate perennials, annuals, grasses, and ferns. In front of the solid brick walls of the house, I would include upright plants, perhaps a small deciduous tree or a banana plant. I would pay special attention to textures and foliage colors. In front of windows, I would make sure that anyone looking out has something worth looking at.

Unlike the typical foundation planting of evergreens, my front border would change with the seasons, as a garden should. I would visit it frequently because something of interest would be going on. Visitors would stroll through this garden and know they are at the home of people with imagination and verve. At least I hope that is what they would think.

Chances are that I will never pursue this dream. Life is short and I have too much to do as it is. But there is a lot to be learned from my troubled past, so here is my best advice:

1. Read labels when buying shrubs. Choose the right plant for the right place.

2. Be skeptical about those labels and do some research, especially if the shrub (or tree) is a major investment. Look at the expected mature size. If I had checked, I would have known my hollies, 'Nana' or not, would grow to six feet or even eight feet and more.

Convince yourself that your foundation planting is a garden too. Where is it written that foundation plants must be lined up in rows? All the same color? The same height? Let my experience be a lesson to all. Do as I say and not as I have done.

Variations on Variegation

I have discovered (about myself as well as about the entire nation of Japan) that it is hard to limit oneself when it comes to variegated plants . . . unless, of course, you do not like them at all. This seems to be the general response: Variegation is something you either like a lot or not at all.

Variegation is a genetic fluke that magically turns ordinary green foliage into leaves striped, edged, or blotched with another color. Usually the variation is white or ecru but it may be shades of yellow or red. A miracle of sorts.

Last spring I attended a lecture by a prominent nurseryman and plant propagator who travels the world collecting plants he thinks will prosper in American gardens. He told us that variegation is a passion, a mania even, among Japanese gardeners, prompting me to confess that I share the obsession and am just a tad guilty of overuse.

I have seen few variegated plants I did not love and covet so, as a result, my garden is full of variegated specimens of all types and sizes: groundcovers, grasses, shrubs, vines, perennials, and, in season, annuals.

If I had space for more trees, I would plant a brace of variegated maples that awed my entire tour group on a visit to England. *Acer crataegifolium* 'Veitchii' has white mottled leaves and is magnificent but, for some reason, has not hit it big in the American market. I suspect they cost a mint.

If you can grow a dogwood, you might consider *Cornus florida* 'Cherokee Daybreak' with green and white foliage, and *Cornus florida* 'Rainbow' whose leaves are edged with gold. Either would be stunning as a single specimen on the lawn or as anchors in a border.

The only thing that keeps me from planting the elegant variegated elderberry, *Sambucus canadensis* 'Variegata,' is that I already have a run-of-the-mill elderberry that flourishes in my woodland garden, and one is quite enough. Eliminating the one I have and enjoy in favor of something more exotic seems too much like discarding an ordinary-looking but sturdy child for a prettier one whose disposition is unknown. We have all heard how deep beauty is, have we not?

But variegated plants are not limited to cutting-edge specimens that tend to break the gardener's bank. Some old favorites, such as *Aucuba japonica,* are common passalong plants that propagate easily from cuttings just about any time of the year. These are the dark green shrubs with yellow splotches on the leaves that look like someone snapped a paintbrush at them. They grow about four or five feet tall and wide and do their best lighting up shady spots.

I have an aucuba in a shaggy shrub border that I really need to do something about one of these days. It is one of those lines of foundation shrubs dug in when you move into a house and regret as soon as all the boxes are unpacked. We have been in our house about forty years, and this border remains the most neglected area of my yard.

The point is that the aucuba thrives in spite of neglect, along with a gardenia, a couple of hydrangeas, some overgrown azaleas, and whatever. You get the shameful picture, I am sure.

A more properly placed aucuba grows in the deep summer shade of a large hickory tree at one end of my long mixed border. Two years ago it was about a foot tall, and it is now almost four feet high and wide. The yellow splotches on the dark green leaves add a much needed bright spot to the corner that it shares with an oakleaf hydrangea, some tropical-looking fatsia, stalky aspidistra, a variegated euonymus, and a tea olive.

This is an attractive mix of shapes and textures. The two variegated plants (the aucuba and the euonymous) in this case work well together even though variegated plants can be tricky to combine, sort of like plaids, stripes, and checks. Sometimes they work; sometimes they do not. Some designers insist that variegated plants be used only as single accents, but far be it from me to set rules of horticultural design. It is your garden. Do what pleases you.

I am especially fond of variegated grasses, and my favorites are *Miscanthus sinensis variegata* with long narrow leaves of green and white, *Miscanthus s.* 'Cabaret' with wider white striping, and *Miscanthus s.* 'Morning Light' with narrower leaves and white midribs. *Miscanthus s.* 'Punktchen' is an upright form of zebra grass whose stripes are horizontal. I suggest you start with several plants of one type placed here and there and see what happens. You can always move them later and probably will.

Some of my favorite groundcovers are white and green pineapple mint, pale green and white lamium, and Bowles' golden sedge, which has yellow grass-like leaves with green margins. These look best next to solid-color shrubs, trees, and perennials. I grow them all in sun and shade and let them wander at will.

Cannas are a good place to start with variegated plants because they are so much more attractive than those with solid-color leaves. I never liked cannas until I saw *Canna* 'Bengal Tiger' and was hooked. Canna blooms look frowsy and disorganized to me, as if they are not sure of the look they are after. I often have the same problem myself.

'Bengal Tiger' has spectacular yellow and green foliage. This is a plant that started off very pricey but can now be found at plant sales as well as in the yards of generous friends. This is not unusual among plants as easily propagated as cannas are. Just dig up a clump and pull it apart.

Hydrangea m. 'Silver V. Mariesii' grows well in almost every garden but mine, it seems. The blooms on this shrub are unspectacular, but the foliage is dynamite: rich green with creamy white leaf margins. *H. m.* 'Lemon Wave' is even more cutting edge: green with yellow edging.

A problem with variegation is that it may be fleeting. Variegated leaves prefer to be green, but the gardener has paid for an attractive mutation and understandably wants to keep what she paid for. The only way to do this is to remove limbs or stems that revert to green. This can be a tedious job and you may give up the effort eventually, but keep it up for a while and enjoy the variegation while you have it.

Variegated combinations are just one more way to make your garden unique and, as with most things horticultural, the variations of variegations are continually changing. Just like gardeners themselves.

A Camellia Is a Camellia Is a Camellia

Throughout fall and winter, I keep a watchful eye from the window over my kitchen sink on a certain no-name camellia growing just outside. Most of the year it is a moderately handsome shrub, nothing to make the gardener's (or dishwasher's) heart beat faster. It is about five feet tall, small by camellia standards, with glossy dark-green leaves. Then, sometime in winter, it bursts into celebration, covered with decorative double red and white blooms. I say "sometime," and I mean it.

No other shrub illustrates the vagaries of winter weather as much as this camellia. Sometimes, depending upon late November temperatures, it begins blooming in mid-December. The table arrangements for Christmas dinner are adorned with camellias in candy cane colors.

Other winters, the camellia is solid green through December, not blooming until January. A freeze turns the blossoms into brown mush. But darned if the camellia does not try again, blooming cheerfully in mid-February.

While my camellia cannot be counted on for Christmas décor, it is a special delight when it does the right thing and blooms in time for seasonal arrangements. But it is also a delight whenever it blooms.

Like most garden experiences, this shrub is a lesson about life. Blossoms that turn into mush are reminders that nature is undependable (though not irresponsible) and we should not complain. When at last they arrive, those red and white February blooms remind us that whatever disaster happens in the garden, there is always next year. Or maybe the year after that.

Completing my personal camellia collection is a tree-sized shrub at the far end of the house. Not many years ago, my husband limbed it up in his usual definitive style with a chainsaw. Not for him the precise and studied pruning of selected limbs. He revs up that machine and has at it. Though I am rarely pleased with the results, he always is.

But, on this occasion, I too was happy. We now have a camellia tree punctuating the back corner of our house. This camellia, also nameless, will be covered in March with large single pinkish-red blooms.

Both my camellias, seedlings no doubt, were given to me at least thirty years ago. Luckily, I planted them on the north side of our house so they grow in predominant shade, which camellias like. I cannot remember ever fertilizing them, and I know I never sprayed or dusted them with an insecticide or fungicide. They have thrived without chemicals or fussiness, as plants should.

Images of camellias appear in ninth-century Chinese artwork. Camellias came to America via Europe from the Orient, possibly as early as the sixteenth century. The first camellias brought to colonial America were *Camellia sinensis,* the tea plant, with hopes of creating an American tea industry.

The ornamental *Camellia japonica* arrived in the late eighteenth century and quickly became popular as a conservatory plant in the Northeast. I have to assume that not many folks had conservatories, so camellia growing was undoubtedly limited to the upper crust. In the early nineteenth century, camellias began to be grown as hardy plants in the South, most notably at Magnolia Gardens and Middleton Place of Charleston, South Carolina, where these shrubs continue to thrive and inspire. A trip to either garden makes it obvious why camellia devotees become addicted.

Like azaleas, camellias grow best in partial shade, so they should be placed in northern or eastern exposures to get them through hot summers. When you plant, incorporate organic material such as shredded pine bark or leaves in the surrounding area. Plant them shallow, with the trunk base slightly above soil level.

Camellias prefer well-drained acidic soil and would be perfectly content growing in finely shredded pine bark or pinestraw compost. They have shallow root systems, so avoid other shallow rooted plants that will compete for moisture and nutrients. Camellias are native to the forests of China, growing as understory shrubs. Keep this point in mind when you consider planting a specimen in full sun.

Camellias seldom need pruning other than minimal shaping or controlling size. Mature camellias can reach ten to fifteen feet and even taller, so read the plant labels carefully before investing time and money on an unwise choice.

While camellias are thought of as Southern shrubs, specific cultivars are grown outdoors successfully as far north as Long Island, New York, on the East Coast, and Washington on the Pacific Coast, as well as in the Midwest.

Camellia flower buds are damaged when temperatures dip to 15 degrees. Open camellias bite the dust when temperatures dip below 26 degrees. Timing of freezing temperatures is critical, as I have learned from the candy cane camellia outside my kitchen.

The key to camellia success is to select cold-hardy plants. I heard recently about a retail nursery having more than forty cultivars in its inventory, and I have read that, incredibly, there are more than 3,000 camellia cultivars. Evidently, camellia breeders have been mighty busy providing something for everyone.

If camellias were scented, my guess is that no one would be paying much attention to roses. After all, even without blooms, camellias are handsome broadleaf evergreens. No rose can make such a claim. Unlike azaleas, which we make such a fuss over, camellias bloom for a six-week period. And, best of all, these gorgeous plants require minimal care and, in my garden, thrive on benign neglect.

An Epiphany in Every Seed

Before I became a gardener, February was the longest month of the year. Of course, at the time, I was a high school English teacher and, for teachers and students alike, February may be short on days but is long on angst.

As a gardener, however, I greet February like an old friend. This is the month that heralds spring. It is time to get my garden rebooted by planting seeds, one of my favorite activities.

I start seeds in plain vermiculite, which can be bought at garden centers in small or very large bags. Either way it is cheap. I make sure to poke holes in the bottoms of my seed-starting containers (recycled cottage cheese cartons or mushroom boxes). I fill the containers to the top with vermiculite and I am ready to begin one of life's great adventures.

Seed packet directions are an excellent resource and I read the advice carefully. After all, seed companies want us to succeed and purchase their products the rest of our lives. For seeds I have harvested myself, and even with commercially packaged seeds, I refer to books that give directions about starting specific plants. The advice varies but isn't that the way with gardeners, especially expert gardeners?

I also consider how and when plants reproduce themselves naturally. Most seeds simply drop to the soil and germinate, as they should. Seeds with hard coats or fleshy coverings can be tricky, but most are manageable. After all, reproduction is their purpose in life.

Place filled containers in a pan of water so the vermiculite sucks up enough moisture to be wet all the way through. The top should be moist, but not soggy. If the seed packet tells me seeds need eight to ten weeks to prepare themselves for outdoor planting, I start them in mid-January. If seeds need six to eight weeks, I start them February 5; two to three weeks, I start them around March 10. Starting dates should be determined by the frost-free date where your garden grows.

This is the hard part: Do not plant the whole packet of seeds unless you really want a hundred zinnias or parsleys. Sprinkle the approximate number of seeds you need, maybe a few extra, over the vermiculite. If seeds are tiny, leave them uncovered; if they are larger, cover them with a layer of vermiculite. In either case, press the top slightly to be sure seeds are in cozy contact with moist vermiculite.

What do you do with all the unplanted seeds? Seal the packet with tape and place in a cool dark place until next year or even the year after that. Contrary to popular opinion, most seeds remain viable for years, as long as they are kept cool. I keep mine in the refrigerator.

Sow one kind of seed per container, even if you are planting just a few seeds from a variety of packets. Seeds germinate at different speeds in different conditions. They also are hard to distinguish in the seedling stage, which leads me to perhaps my most important advice: Label each container with at least the name of the plant. I also indicate the seed company and special requirements such as light and temperature.

My seedlings have never suffered from damp-off or other fungal diseases, and I believe I owe this good fortune to vermiculite and the rapidity with which my seedlings emerge. I place the containers in a warm spot (in a particularly warm room, on a towel-covered electric blanket, on top of an appliance, near a wood stove, or even on top of a grow-light). Catalogs offer heating cables and pads to perk up germination, but they tend to be costly and I prefer to spend my money on plants.

This is the truth: Most seedlings emerge within two or three days. The packets might tell you eight days or thirty days, but, as a rule, I get them going before a week is up. The first thing I do when I get up in the morning, before making coffee or letting the dogs out, is check my seedlings. If even one or two seedlings have popped through the vermiculite, the whole container is placed immediately under a grow-light or in a sunny, warm window.

I advise you to purchase or build a grow-light. After I ordered one from a catalog, my husband built a better one for a pittance and in a jiffy. The one he built has two shelves (like a bookcase) with light fixtures facing downward. I use cheap fluorescent shop lights with happy results. The grow-light sits in the laundry room and, when not in use for starting seeds, it provides useful shelving for yard shoes and other stuff.

Some seeds have special requirements. Currently I have two containers in my refrigerator: one with mimulus seeds and the other with columbine seeds. In a warm spot (under the woodstove, a relic from the eighties that we still enjoy) is a container of alstroemeria seeds that first had to be soaked for twenty-four hours. If they do not emerge in three weeks, I am supposed to refrigerate them for three weeks. It is a bit of trouble but alstroemerias are worth the effort.

I do not fertilize while seeds are germinating. The seed carries sufficient nutrients within itself to get the growing process started. Once seedlings develop leaves, many seed starters water with a weak fertilizing solution. I do not. After seedlings are transferred to separate containers of potting mix and start looking hungry, I fertilize with a weak solution of fish emulsion.

Why bother with seeds? For one thing, you probably will not find alstroemerias or asarinas or heteropappus in your local garden center. Also, by starting from seeds, you can have fifty columbines for the price of a single plant at a nursery.

But the best reason for starting seeds is to experience the growing process from seed to bloom. Seed starting is not just an exercise in frugality (which I heartily applaud) but is also an adventure of the spirit. The emergence of each seedling is a small epiphany to savor.

An Epiphany in Every Seed

It's Dangerous Out There in the Garden

Holy moly! If you plan to murder someone, look no further than your garden. At a recent conference, I picked up a brochure about poisonous plants and was astounded by the length of the list and the presence of toxic flora in my own borders.

Most everyone knows about oleander. Legend has it that Women Loyal to the South offered a tea made of oleander leaves to certain men in blue. Since we all know women are the kinder, gentler sex, I assume this is a myth, but beware of salad bowls made of oleander wood, no matter how gracious your hostess seems.

Beware also of unidentified leaves or flowers in your salad as well. If they resemble azalea leaves or blooms, remove them before you chomp. In fact, you might want to remove yourself from the table after warning other diners. (Do not even consider offering your portion to anyone else, no matter how despicable.) Azalea leaves and flowers are toxic, and so is azalea honey. I will not elaborate on the effects, but they are not pleasant.

I have long known about the toxicity of castor bean plants (*Ricinus communis*) but grow them anyway. Mine have deep burgundy leaves. I limit the plant to a single stem and strip the lower leaves so, by the Fourth of July, I have castor bean trees rising above my borders, adding purple punch to the color scheme.

Surprisingly, castor bean leaves and seedpods are not lethal, as I had previously thought, but you will not feel well for a while after a castor bean snack. You will not want to leave home either. I suggest you avoid throwing the leaves into the stew or chewing on the spiky little pods as you stroll around the garden, especially since there are more flavorful alternatives.

Perhaps in the interest of saving lives, I should be more graphic. If you nibble on daphne, you can expect "vesication and edema [*i.e.,* blistering and swelling] of the lips and oral cavity" and serious aches in the tummy. Take heed of this warning and leave the daphne alone.

I have a careless habit of holding cuttings in my mouth before sticking them into rooting hormone. Sure enough, after reading the warnings, my lips felt distinctly vesicated and edemic until I washed my mouth out. I resolve to mend my ways.

You probably have heard about the dangers of angel's trumpet (*Datura*), a handsome plant with trumpet-like blooms. It is an annual that reseeds readily.

Speaking of these seeds, which come packaged in a sphere that looks like a spikey cannonball, they are the most toxic part of the plant.

Before you go out and rip out your oleanders, castor beans, daphne, datura, and, yes, even your azaleas, do not think your garden will then be safe. You can still expect to be plenty uncomfortable after snacking on amaryllis, bleeding heart, hellebores, delphiniums, English ivy, English holly, foxglove, and iris.

Guess what else is on the poisonous plants list. Irish potatoes! The potatoes are safe, but the vines, sprouts, green skin, and foliage may make life unpleasant. I am sure, in my ignorance, I have eaten a sprout or two while munching on raw potatoes.

The leaflet I am using as a resource advises, "Use antidotes accordingly and with caution." I find this advice scary and intend to be more careful about my snacks.

Most of us know about the dangers of mistletoe, but not many have been made aware of the toxicity of lantana, lilies, lupine, morning glories, mountain laurel, monkshood, moon vine, and rhubarb leaves.

Do not think you are safe indoors either. Philodendron will do a mean number on your mouth and throat and is toxic to cats who need to be warned. Poinsettias, in spite of being a symbol of Christmas spirit, will also make you mighty sick. I do not know what they will do to kitty.

We have been warned about the dangers of tobacco and have quit smoking forever, but it turns out that a chew or two of flowering tobacco (*Nicotiana tabacum*) will cause tremors, collapse, and respiratory failure. The list indicates EMERGENCY CONDITION (as it also does in the notes about azaleas) so if you are going to do any ripping out of plants, azaleas and nicotiana are the two I would start with.

Winding up the list are wisteria, yellow jessamine, and yew, all of which cause symptoms that give me tremors to think about.

It's Dangerous Out There in the Garden

The list I have been studying came from the College of Veterinary Medicine at Iowa State University in Ames, Iowa, but I assume the clinical signs may be experienced by all mammals whether we walk on two legs or four.

I have had dogs all my gardening life and have never seen them graze on the leaves, flowers, or stems of plants other than grass. Could it be that dogs and other critters do not need a list to know they should not chew questionable plants? And why do we humans not have the same innate access to this information?

Children love the outdoors. At least I hope they still do. They are curious and they love to pretend. I recall growing up in California and playing tea party with lantana blooms and berries. My playmates and I survived, but it does give me pause.

The fact is that many poisonous plants have alluring seedpods, flowers, and leaves that lend themselves to children's play and imagination.

We need to make sure that children (and certain adults I know) are warned to never ever eat anything they do not see their mother or father or other trusted adult chewing and swallowing. Friends do not count since they have no more sense than your own child does.

Garden to your heart's content but do not nibble on leaves, berries, bark, and other plant parts. The life you save may be your own, and saving the life of a gardener improves the world immeasurably.

To Prune or Not to Prune

To prune or not to prune. That is the question, and the answers are varied as well as confusing. I have two basic rules for this job myself: Prune after bloom is the first, and the second is prune when the urge hits because who knows when it will strike again?

While the primary purpose of deadheading is to remove seed-heads or spent flowers to assure repeated bloom, the purpose of pruning is to reshape shrubs and trees to stimulate foliage growth and to control size as well as structure.

If you followed my advice in the fall and left buddleias and lantanas to wither as winter interest, I applaud you, especially if you normally regard neatness as a virtue. I leave everything pretty much as is in the fall, putting off cleanup until I need space.

I was delighted when a landscape designer who really knows her stuff showed me her garden in December. It looked as disheveled as mine. She assured me that the English leave their gardens to loll around all winter in their natural state, and that is recommendation enough for me. I have seen how those gardens look come spring.

February is late winter where I garden, and this is the official time to consider cutting back buddleias, lantanas, and other summer flowering shrubs. It is not a bad idea to wait until mid-March but, if your patience has been used up, cut them back now to about seven inches from the ground.

Do not prune mophead, lacecap, or oakleaf hydrangeas until they start leafing out and then just thin the old stems out and tip-prune here and there. Too little is better than too much. Here is the big "however," however: Hydrangeas that bloom on new wood, such as 'Annabelle' and 'Tardiva,' should be cut to the ground just like buddleias and lantanas.

I write in a calendar, which I use as a gardening journal, what to prune when, or I would never remember which hydrangeas bloom on new wood. I also would not remember when to lime, fertilize, or anything else. It is all I can do to remember where I left my clippers fifteen minutes ago.

Other shrubs to prune now are sasanquas, hollies, boxwood, ligustrum, cleyera, abelia, barberry, clethra, and vitex. Actually, you can prune any shrub you own as long as you realize that, if the plant blooms in the spring, you will be cutting off flowers. That is why I am a member of the prune-after-bloom school.

Once you decide something must be pruned, the next decision is what surgical procedure to use. Tip-pruning is the gentlest. Just look over the plant and trim branches that are headed in the wrong direction or have grown too long.

Make your cuts just above a branch, leaf, or an outside bud and cut each stem at an angle. Tip-pruning retains the natural shape of the plant but will encourage side-branching, making it bushier.

Shearing is an even-surface pruning, kind of like a marine's haircut. If you want a formal hedge or shrubs in the shape of balls and boxes, you will need to cut the plants to the desired height, allowing space for this year's growth. Then cut back the sides evenly, again leaving room for this year's growth.

As you shear, slope the sides to make the top of the plant narrower than the bottom so sunlight will reach the lower branches. Otherwise, your hedge will be leggy and bare at the nether parts. Shearing is not for the lazy or faint of heart and, frankly, life is too short for me to attempt it.

If you have admired sheared hedges on great estates, remember the size of their gardening staffs. Also, the gardeners use wire frames to guide their cuts. As you think it over, ask yourself why God made a point of not shaping plants like balls and squares.

Thinning is the third pruning procedure. When you thin a plant, you remove entire old stems or unwanted branches where they emerge from the main trunk or the ground. This method preserves the natural shape of the plant and rejuvenates older plants, letting in sunlight and providing space for new growth.

A fourth pruning procedure, less elegant than the other three, is one most gardeners do eventually. The urge is sometimes irresistible. In fact, this is what I advised you do to your buddleia and lantana. This procedure is called "stooling" or "coppicing," and you simply lop the plant off near ground level and let it start over.

I have coppiced hollies, azaleas, weigelia, mock orange, spirea, and various other plants, and they all seemed to enjoy the experience. So did I. It is kind of cleansing, and, unlike shearing, the process is not tricky.

I tend to be a minimalist with gardening tools. To do any pruning, I use by-pass clippers and loppers. I use hedge clippers for deadheading perennials and annuals, but that is another chapter. For the tough stuff, I use my husband, who is handy with a pruning saw. He uses a chain saw to prune if I do not keep my eye on him.

I am also minimalist about pruning. In general, I like plants that look the way nature intends. I cannot wait for my ligustrum hedge to be thick and fifteen feet tall to give shelter to the birds and privacy to me. On the other hand, I have two hollies and a buddleia I trim as trees. I leave my crepe myrtles alone except for a nip here and there to keep the trunks bare and to encourage reblooming.

Whatever you do about pruning, do what appeals to you and not what you think is "correct." Your garden is your kingdom and you get to make or break all the rules if you choose. No wonder we gardeners are such a contented lot.

CHAPTER 4

Spring

Every day of spring is a rebirth. I can hardly wait to get into the garden each morning to see what surprises have emerged.

It's Spring . . . and Time to Shop

When daytime temperatures hover close to 70 degrees, my gardening juices flow. Early spring has arrived. I am ready to play in the dirt, and folks with plants to sell rub their hands together in anticipation.

Who can blame them? Visions of lush, nonstop blooms dance in gardeners' heads. We itch to fill space with color and scent. First-year gardener or horticultural sophisticate, we are ready to shop.

Far be it from me to offer advice about how to shop for clothes. Just last week I wandered around three major stores and twelve departments. After walking miles from one "designer area" to another, I picked out four garments that may or may not fit either my body or my life. None of the four items I wound up buying was quite what I was looking for, nor did any of them inspire me to purchase five more just like it.

Nurseries are quite another story. I know what I am doing there. I know the colors that lure me, the size plants that will fit into my border, and the unmistakable signs of quality. The plants I buy are precisely what I want (even if I do not know it until I see them) and, unless the plant of choice is large or pricey, I might buy three or five or seven so they make a statement.

Furthermore, unlike department stores, at nurseries all like items are massed together. Shrubs are in one area, perennials in another, herbs in still another, and annuals side-by-side in their own section. They are even divided into sun and shade areas.

A shopper does not have to walk across the nursery to compare coreopsis and coneflowers. The hostas are neighbors, so it is easy to see how their variegated leaves vary. The difference between *Loropetalum chinense* 'Hillier' and *Loropetalum chinense rubrum* 'Blush' is right before your eyes.

While I may be helpless in choosing clothes, I am a wily shopper when it comes to plant buying. My advice: Do your shopping at a reputable garden center. I prefer places where I can talk to the owner if I wish, where plants are guaranteed, and where salespeople are gardeners, not indifferent clerks.

I like to converse with folks who love plants. Watch them talk about a particular plant. If they stroke the foliage as if it were a puppy and their eyes sparkle, you can trust what they say. If their eyes glaze and they seem bored with their merchandise, take your money and your trust elsewhere.

If I suspect a plant is rootbound or its roots are sickly, I upend the pot and look at what is happening under cover. Would you buy a dress without looking at the buttonholes and seams? A pound of bacon without raising the flap? When you buy a plant, the most important part you are paying for is the rootball. That is where the future lies.

If the salesperson objects to my snooping, I smile graciously, put the plant down, and hold on to my cash. Now, understand that most container-grown plants are a little rootbound. They look their best when their roots fill the pot and their thoughts turn to foliage-production. I certainly want a plant that is sufficiently rooted to be ready to focus its energy on foliage and bloom once I get it in the ground.

If the roots fill the pot and are somewhat entwined, the plant goes in my shopping cart. If the roots are badly knotted and soggy brown, and the pot is essentially empty of soil, I leave the plant for some less particular customer.

When purchasing annuals and perennials, I choose plants that are not in bloom. I want roots, not flowers. Flowers fade, but the roots will be with me the rest of the plant's life. Nursery people tend to rush the blooms because color sells. The blooming plant may have been in the pot too long, so the roots are stressed and weak.

Once again, upend the pot and check the roots. Are they white and healthy-looking? Or brown and mushy? Have they been overwatered? In the pot too long? Whether the plant is a 50-cent annual or a $50 tree, roots matter most.

Do I ever buy straggly plants that have outgrown their pots? Rootbound plants? Plants in full bloom? Of course I do. If they are on sale and I think they are salvageable, I am as happy with a bargain as the next gardener. I may be setting myself up for disappointment, but life is full of risks worth taking, especially at half-price.

When I purchase a less-than-perfect tree or shrub or perennial, I repot it in potting mix and compost. The new pot should be three or four inches larger than what the plant has been growing in, and I tease or even slice the roots loose before covering them. The potting mix (in contrast to garden and potting soils) assures good drainage, which is what the plant needs most at this point. Do not fertilize. The search for nourishment stimulates root growth, so you want to keep the plant on the hungry side.

If the foliage is mature, I cut the plant back by at least one-third and put it in a shady spot. When it starts putting out new growth, I move it into morning sun and let it rest at least a month and perhaps a full season before placing it in its permanent location, depending upon its progress and my patience.

Some gardeners have separate "hospital beds" where they place stressed plants, but I prefer to keep the patients in pots in locations I visit regularly. If the plant starts looking diseased or hopeless, I get rid of it and hope I have learned something from the experience.

Perhaps that is what draws us to gardening. There is always something to learn. We grow gardens but we also grow ourselves, so a gardener's life is full, not of just risk but of discovery and delight.

If You Plant Them, They Will Bloom

PERENNIALS

What I like best about perennials is their resilience. Up they come, year after year, surprising me with their ability to withstand freezing temperatures, droughts, and downpours. What they do not bounce back from, however, is complete neglect. Perennials need a little tender loving care, but we gardeners are well rewarded for minimal effort.

My main border is a mixture of trees, shrubs, vines, herbs, perennials, and annuals. The soil in this area works hard almost all year since my expectations are unflagging and I count on lots of bloom from early spring until hard freeze. It seems only fair that I occasionally pamper the soil at the beginning of the growing season.

The most thorough way to revitalize soil is to remove old perennials from a particular area, add amendments, dig them into the top eight to twelve inches of the soil, and then replant. If you are a glutton for labor, you can double-dig, which means you remove the top twelve inches of soil, dig the undersoil to loosen it another twelve inches, and then replace the top soil and mix in the amendments. I have never done this myself.

Double-digging makes better sense if your soil is clay or hard-packed. To tell the truth, I do not even single-dig. I just cover an area with newspaper, compost and mulch, and wait a season or two. The soil becomes friable, the grass and weeds become compost, and I am ready to plant.

I do amend my soil on occasion with organic materials such as compost, kelp meal, alfalfa pellets, cottonseed meal, and blood meal. I dig up perennials about every three years, divide them, and amend that particular soil before replanting. The years in between I just scratch in amendments around plants, according to whim rather than plan.

To divide perennials, dig the plant up, wash off the soil, and ease the plant apart. If easing does not do the job, use a large sharp knife to cut through the root tangle. Each division should have roots attached. Before replanting the baby in the garden or in a pot, trim the roots a bit to stimulate growth.

Spring is the optimum time to divide perennials that bloom in late summer or fall. Wait until fall to divide spring perennials. Although you will not kill the plant if you divide at the wrong time, it may pout a bit, depriving you of blooms for a season.

Late-summer perennials to consider dividing in spring (if they look tired and overgrown) include salvias, patrinia, veronica, coreopsis, coneflowers, physostegia, yarrow, and sedums. Fall-blooming perennials such as chrysanthemums, asters, goldenrod, and swamp sunflowers should also be divided in spring.

Swamp sunflower (*Helianthus angustifolius*) is a super plant, both in size and survivability. Plant it in the back of a border or in a space of its own. I cut mine back by half on the Fourth of July to keep it manageable, and it still reaches six feet by October when it blooms. In spite of its name, swamp sunflower puts on a really big show in dry sandy soil. I cannot imagine what it does in a bog.

I crave continuous daisies, spring through fall, so I grow them all: ox-eyes, nippons, shastas, and, best of all, Becky's daisy (*Chrysanthemum xsuperbum* 'Becky'). Becky is a tall daisy with four- to five-inch nonstop blooms, strong stems that do not flop over the way shastas do, and tolerable year-round foliage.

My all-time favorite perennials are delicate-looking columbines, both natives and fancy hybrids. Columbine foliage (which stays a lovely gray-green all winter) is often attacked by leaf-miners, but I ignore the symptoms and the problem solves itself without damage to the plant. Columbines are tougher than they look. When the foliage becomes ragged, I cut it to the ground and new young sprouts emerge.

Another prized staple in my garden is bright orange butterfly weed (*Asclepias tuberosa*). A native prairie plant, asclepias reaches weed status in some areas because it is a prolific seeder. I would be thrilled if asclepias seeded heavily in my garden, and Monarch butterflies would be even happier. This all-purpose milkweed provides nectar, a place to lay eggs, and a food source for their caterpillars.

Perennials I treasure are considerably more heat-tolerant than the gardener. They demand little and give generously from early spring to that first hard freeze that now seems far away. Water well a couple of times a week until plants are established and start putting out new growth. Do not forget to mulch.

Keep in mind that perennials are in your garden for the long haul. At least that is what you hope. Since perennials may take a while to feel at home, do not fret if they do not flower the first year or much the second year. If you plant them, blooms will come.

ANNUALS

While the major portion of my gardener's heart belongs to perennials and flowering shrubs, I admit that nothing fluffs up a garden like annuals. I love the color and dependability of these troopers that keep on blooming in spite of heat, drought, and neglect, aware they have but one season to strut their stuff before going on to the great garden beyond.

Perennials and flowering shrubs are more sedate in their flowering, usually giving their all for a brief period and then just hanging around the rest of the year. They get the most attention and the best soil but, like favored children, they know they do not have to be terrific over the long haul to be adored. Annuals, on the other hand, work hard for a living and deserve more respect.

107

Most annuals I plant are started from seed indoors sometime between January and mid-April, depending upon germination requirements. I am unlucky or unskilled at starting seeds in the garden itself. I forget where I put them, I am negligent about keeping them watered, and the birds find them delectable.

Cleome is a good example. I have attempted to start cleomes in various locations, assuming they are Annuals for Dummies since other gardeners gripe about cleome seedlings coming up everywhere with no effort on the gardener's part. But not in my garden, a reminder that consistent results are not to be expected in nature or anywhere else in life.

Even easy-as-pie zinnias are started indoors for my gardening pleasure. I prefer daisy-type zinnias to the voluptuous ruffled varieties. Butterflies like them better, too, since the flat surface serves as a landing site and rest area while they dine royally on zinnia nectar. I plant zinnias here and there wherever I need some color or can squeeze them in.

If You Plant Them, They Will Bloom

My favorite zinnia is the low-growing *Z. angustifolia,* which comes in orange, gold, and white. They are extraordinarily heat- and drought-tolerant and remain perky until heavy frost if I keep them deadheaded.

I cannot imagine a summer garden without tithonia, or Mexican sunflower, which grows five or six feet tall and almost as wide. Tithonia has abundant red-orange blooms that lure butterflies with seductive abandon. Inevitably they fall over in a summer downpour but turn their faces bravely to the sun and continue to grow upward. Since I discovered this resilience, I look forward to their change in direction.

Another regular is melampodium, a shrub-like annual that works well as a front-of-the-border landscape plant or spotted here and there in a mixed border. This sturdy golden bloomer tolerates heat, drought, and frost. Buy a plant or two, save seeds at the end of the season, and you can have cost-free melampodiums forever.

My usual method of planting annuals is to walk around the yard looking for an open spot where I can squeeze in a plant or two. I try to consider color but, after a while, all I am thinking about is finding space. When I locate a planting site, I dig up the soil with a trowel, toss in some compost, pop in the plants, and water if the soil is dry.

To keep annuals blooming, deadhead regularly. This means removing blossoms after they dry up. I deadhead both annuals and perennials with hedge clippers, whacking the plant back by one-quarter to one-third. The plants look a little mangled but quickly put out more foliage and blooms.

If you do not deadhead, your plants think they are through for the year. They have reproduced themselves with seeds and are ready to go on vacation. Do not let them get away with such slothfulness . . . even if it means you cannot be slothful yourself.

Spring

The Hydrangea Puzzlement

Without a doubt, the garden question I am asked most frequently is "When do I prune my hydrangeas?" Often the person asking has already cut them down because they looked unkempt after losing their leaves last fall. What the inquirer really wants me to say is "You've done it just right." I wish that were always my answer.

Earlier in my life, I knew the answer to the hydrangea question and could say confidently that the gardener should prune hydrangeas late in the winter, cutting out one-third of the oldest canes as well as any dead wood. The wood is obviously dead because it is not leafing out. Pretty easy decision there. From the remaining canes, remove old flower heads, cutting back just above the final pair of new buds.

Then, around the Fourth of July, you might prune the hydrangea more emphatically to shape it up or restrict its size. In fact, if your hydrangea is overgrown or tired looking, you could whack it off at ground level. Whatever you do in July, the shrub will have enough time to produce new branches that harden off before the first freeze.

Here's the rub: The process I have described is appropriate for bigleaf hydrangeas (*Hydrangea macrophylla*) and oakleaf hydrangeas (*Hydrangea quercifolia*), but even with them the rule is not consistent. I visited a garden recently and saw a very large oakleaf hydrangea that the owner cuts to the ground every winter. He swears it blooms vigorously, though he has removed every bit of old wood he can.

To make matters more confusing, we have panicle hydrangeas (*Hydrangea paniculata*) with irresistible white cone-shaped inflorescences that bloom from mid- to late summer. The blooms are gorgeous and creamy white for a couple of months and then they dry to a Martha Stewart green. If you are a hydrangeaphile, you have to have one of these in your garden. Or perhaps a dozen.

Another allure of the panicle hydrangeas is that they like sun. Maybe not full sun, but my much-prized *H. paniculata* 'Tardiva' is in the back of a mixed border that gets morning shade and afternoon sun. (How's that for good planning?) Those 'Tardiva' blooms that show up in mid- to late summer are on canes that began growing in early spring. Obviously, you want as much new wood as possible, and the best way to stimulate growth is to cut the hydrangeas down to the ground in late winter.

Just to show you how inconsistent Mother Nature can be, one panicle hydrangea ('Praecox,' a large early-flowering peegee) should be pruned after blooming, like the bigleaf and oakleaf hydrangeas. Early flowering is the deciding factor.

Chances are, if you are not sure what kind of hydrangeas you have, they are the old-fashioned bigleaf shrubs. They may be mopheads or they may be lacecaps, but they are probably *macrophylla*, especially if someone gave them to you or you bought them at a plant sale.

The reason I say this is because until recently panicles have not been popular or widely available unless you really went hunting and did not mind spending the grocery money on your garden. They have since come down in price and are sold at most nurseries. My 'Tardiva,' for instance, was $20 and I had to order it from a catalog, but I have seen it recently at local nurseries for $12.

But there is more to a gardener's life than hydrangea shrubs. There are hydrangea vines, both deciduous and evergreen. Even better is Japanese climbing hydrangea (*Schizophragma hydrangeoides*), which grows faster and blooms sooner than the classic climbing hydrangea, *H. anomala ssp. petiolaris*.

When I saw a photograph of *S. hydrangeoides* 'Moonlight,' I was awestruck. As I write, one sits at the base of a large hickory tree that it will begin to climb this spring if all goes well. And, if all goes really really well, it will eventually bear white, flat-topped inflorescences, eight to ten inches wide. The catalog claimed, "Were it never to bloom the foliage alone is dazzling." How could I resist?

But back to the Big Question: When do I prune? It probably comes as no surprise that over the years, I have amassed a collection of hydrangeas. I no longer know offhand who some of them are, let alone remember when they bloom.

I solved this problem a few years ago by making a rough drawing of my garden beds where hydrangeas reside. I indicate each shrub with a circle, jotting down its name if I know it, as well as when it blooms. In my gardening calendar, in the appropriate month, I jot a list of the hydrangeas that need pruning at that time.

I cut hydrangeas that bloom on new wood close to the ground in late February or early March. The more new wood generated, the better. Hydrangeas that bloom on old wood do not get trimmed until after their early summer bloom, giving them ample time to generate stems and buds for the following spring.

Do I sometimes get confused? Of course. Does the world end if I prune at the wrong time? Not that I have noticed.

Once again we are reminded of why we garden. No matter what mistakes we make, hydrangeas regrow, new shrubs are just a garden center away, and another cultivar is out there, calling our name.

The Hydrangea Puzzlement

Turning Yard Work into Garden Joy

Dutch iris are blooming in my garden and so are yellow woods poppies and dwarf veronica. A few violets peek out, forget-me-nots are in full flower, and candytuft makes a crisp white edge in the shrub border. The earliest spireas do indeed look like bridal wreaths, and Lady Banksia rose climbs over an unused clothesline and takes my breath away.

This has to be the most energizing time in the garden, full of promise and rebirth and surprise . . . and so much to accomplish.

I never clean out my borders in the fall, preferring to let things die a natural death, preserving stalks and seedheads for the birds, wildlife cover, and winter interest. I am all for winter interest and conservation, since they are not only good for the environment but also justify postponement of cleaning up.

But tidying the garden in spring is not work at all. With greenery popping up and out, my clean-up juices flow and I happily crawl around on my hands and knees, pulling back mulch, urging weeds to leave the premises, and finding babies to pot up for friends' gardens as well as my own.

I meditate as I cut brittle stems sticking up from emerging leaves. I trim buddleia to the ground or into tree shapes. I pinch new growth to stimulate branching and shape up the ligustrum hedge so the top is narrower than the bottom, letting sunlight reach bottom foliage.

I need to dig up overcrowded daffodils but put it off until late April when the foliage begins to die back. I have lots of places for the dug-up bulbs so I mark my calendar, reminding myself to get the job done before the foliage disappears and I lose track of their locations.

For instance, I write in the April 15 space "Dig up daffodils" since that will be more than six weeks after bloom, time enough for them to fatten up to produce next spring's crop. I intend to replant the bulbs immediately in the ground so I jot down the areas where they should go, as well as the names of people to whom promises have been made.

I have tried storing bulbs in a cool dry place and planting them in the fall, but wonder what is the point when they could spend their summer building their characters in the heat and humidity as the rest of us do.

I trim azaleas right after they bloom so they spend the summer developing buds for next year's flowers. Once they finish dazzling us with their blossoms, azaleas are easy to overlook. Taking time to cut them back pays off in fuller and healthier foliage. I am unsure what it does to their character.

Abelia too needs to be cut back. I have a row of old-fashioned glossy abelias between my mixed border and woodland garden. I cut back the oldest branches to the ground and the rest of the branches randomly by one-third to one-half.

After mock orange and weigela bloom, they will be "stooled" (British for whacked off at ground level) to keep them shapely and to stimulate next year's bloom. Since stooling is hard on the plant as well as the gardener, I do this job only every five years. Both shrubs recover quickly.

The only way I can remember which year to do the stooling is to mark my calendar when the deed is done. When I start next year's calendar, I will transfer the note as a reminder not to do it that year but to wait until the following year or the year after that. I will spend the intervening time looking for someone to do it for me. Someone with a chainsaw and strong shoulders.

Once the mixed borders are cleaned out and I am back to bare earth, I may distribute compost or other soil amendments. Sometimes I do and sometimes I do not, depending primarily on gut feeling rather than scientific analysis. I do believe in soil tests, especially for folks just starting their gardens. But, if you garden organically over a decade or so, you create a balanced environment that usually takes care of itself in regard to nutrients as well as insects and disease.

I mulch with hay purchased by the roll bale. The borders look odd until the plants fill in, but my neighbors and I have become used to the look and regard it as one more rite of spring. The hay decays much faster than pinestraw or shredded bark and becomes part of the soil. Over the years my once pallid sand has become dark, nutritious loam you want to sink your hands into just for the pleasure of its company.

In the meantime, the mulch discourages weeds and keeps the soil temperature warmer now but, during the summer months, cooler and moist. The mulch in an established border starts out about four to six inches thick, but rain and time settle it down.

The trick to gardening, at least the gardening I choose to do, is to focus on pleasurable endeavors. If a task is hard and tedious, think of a way to make it easier or do not do it at all. There is always a way to turn yard work into garden joy, and we should make sure we find it.

Reba and Me in the Garden

I found myself riveted to the television set as I watched a newswoman interview country singer Reba McIntyre. I do not listen to much country music unless I am locked in a truck with my husband zipping up or down I-95. Better Willie Nelson than some political zealot, to my way of thinking.

I was absolutely charmed by Reba who has garnered multiple Grammies, starred in a sitcom bearing her name, and wowed Broadway in a revival of *Annie Get Your Gun*. It is not easy to wow New York theatergoers but Reba has been called "the ultimate Annie," a remarkable feat considering her predecessors in the role. But I digress.

Here is how Reba caught my attention. This woman obviously has it all, including great looks, business savvy, and charm. The interviewer wondered what was left to accomplish. "What else would you like to do?" she asked.

Reba's answer: "I'd like to have a garden." Those of us who garden know exactly what she meant. A garden is a world of one's own and the satisfaction gained from planning, planting, and growing cannot be surpassed by any other human endeavor. Child raising is admittedly more rewarding, as a rule, but the tribulations can be harrowing. Gardening problems are easily solved. Just rip out the offending or sickly plant and start over.

Starting over is what spring is about. Every day brings new delights, and I can hardly wait to get out into the garden each morning to see what surprises have emerged. Just when I decide to pull out the bearded iris because they take up too much room and fall over in the rain, I am greeted by a dozen breathtaking purple blooms that make me revise my intentions and consider planting more.

As I pull out overgrown groundcovers, I discover tiny ferns I had forgotten. When I cut back dried stems of perennials, I find small green shoots coming up. And, of course, the nurseries are full of fresh temptations. When I buy plants, I select those with the most potential for dividing or propagating. For instance, I purchased a six-inch pot of red switchgrass (*Panicum virgatum* 'Shenandoah,') that grows three feet tall and is supposed to turn really really red by midsummer. I paid $8 for the pot but, when I checked its roots, I discovered I could divide the plant into four or five sections, making it a terrific bargain.

I also bought *Sedum* 'Purple Emperor' and snipped four cuttings before planting the mother in a dry sunny spot. According to the catalog, this twelve- to fifteen-inch sedum has leaves that the catalog promises "range from purple-blue . . . to rich burgundy." (Notice a trend here? I am really into red foliage this year.) For the hefty initial price of $10, I garnered five plants plus lots of cuttings to come.

Few plant purchases go into my garden without being divided or propagated. In addition, I am always snipping away or digging up and dividing mature plants. I cannot imagine the day will ever come when I say, "I have enough plants. No more." But, if it does, the pleasure of sharing plants with friends or contributing to plant sales will remain.

For the price of a seed packet, I produced over 100 Thai basil plants. Probably ten went into my own garden and the rest were distributed to friends and given to the church rummage sale.

At no cost at all, I collected seeds last fall from a burgundy castor bean plant (*Ricinus communis*) and produced another 100 plants. Five or six went into my garden, and the rest went to a plant sale and friends.

Dividing plants involves washing off most of the dirt from the roots and pulling the plant apart. If the plant cannot be pulled apart, cut the root mass into pieces with a sharp butcher knife or small saw. You can plant the pieces directly into your garden, or you can pot each one in potting mix (not garden dirt) and save them for later use.

To propagate cuttings, make a rooting box out of four boards or use a rectangular plastic container with extra drainage holes. I used to use a bottomless wooden rooting box permanently located under a large shade tree, but now most of my propagating is done in four or five plastic containers, light enough to move around.

The medium with which you fill your container is a matter of choice . . . but one of the choices is *not* garden dirt, even if it seems like pure sand. Some propagators swear by perlite, an organic material that looks like small styrofoam pellets. I depend upon coarse and gritty builder's sand. Still others use a packaged peat-based potting mix. The purposes of medium are to hold the cuttings upright and to retain consistent moisture.

Take four- to six-inch cuttings that are firm but not woody. Make the cut just below a growing node (the bump on the stem), remove all but the top four to six leaves, and stick the cut end into water and then rooting hormone (such as Hormonex or Rootone). Poke a hole in the medium with a pencil or stick or finger, insert the cutting, and firm the medium around it, like tucking in a baby.

In a couple of weeks, the cuttings will start producing roots. You can tell this is true by tugging the cutting upward. If it does not yield, you have a rooted plant that you should pot up for a few months before moving it to the garden. If the cutting slides out of the medium without resistance, push it back down, tuck it in, and wait another few weeks. As long as the cutting remains green and perky, there is hope.

It amazes me to learn that many accomplished gardeners resist the joys of creating their own plant supply. Not only do seed starting, propagating, and dividing provide an abundance of cost-free plants. They are satisfying activities that get us close to the earth where gardeners belong.

Reba and Me in the Garden

Put the Xip into Xeriscaping

Last night it rained, the first time in weeks. The grass is already turning beige although summer has not even begun. Hydrangeas droop by midafternoon and perennials threaten to expire. Meteorologists warn us simultaneously of hot dry conditions, interrupted by more than our share of hurricanes. What is a poor gardener to do?

What a poor gardener is *not to do* is to give up gardening. Our gardens bring too much pleasure and too much healthful physical activity for us to throw in our trowels. We just need to garden smarter by xeriscaping (pronounced zeer-eh-scaping), creating attractive borders or landscapes that need less water.

Before you picture a swath of pea gravel and a bunch of cactus, let me assure you that a xeriscaped garden will not be obvious to anyone but gardeners-in-the-know who recognize your intelligence and creativity and applaud your frugality. A xeriscaped garden looks just like a garden should, full of color, green foliage, and healthy soil.

By now, your garden may be completely planted and possibly you have already reached the point of saying, "Oh well, maybe next year." But xeriscaping can be begun at any time of the year. You may have to move some plants, but if they are not thriving where they are, what have you got to lose?

For those of you who have your own wells, do not get too complacent. Wells run dry if the drought persists long enough. We have a friend in Florida who has a well but is still allowed to water only once a week. The sprinkler police are quick to pounce on water wastrels, and neighbors tend to get tough when the grass gets greener over the property line.

By following the principles of xeriscaping, you will improve your garden's chances of surviving La Niña and whatever else lies ahead.

Step one: Rethink your garden plan by grouping plants according to water needs. Instead of giving up perennials and annuals that require intensive moisture, plant them in one or two "hydrozones" to concentrate water use. You will not only save water but you will save time as well by focusing hose-time. Most gardeners begrudge the hours wasted dragging hoses around when we could be lying in a hammock pondering the universe.

As you plan, observe over the course of the day the movement of the sun and shade and make an hourly chart. You may be surprised to discover that patterns have shifted because of tree growth or other factors. Plant your moisture-neediest where they will get shade in the hottest part of the day, the afternoon.

Plant your toughest, most drought-resistant specimens in the toughest sites. Makes sense, doesn't it?

Can you actually move plants when the air is hot and the soil dry? Of course you can. These are your plants and your garden. Your garden may be the only area in your life where you have total control. You are the decision-maker, the top banana, the CEO, the Queen or King.

When moving plants (which I do all the time), I lower the risks by waiting for rain and then making the transfer at dusk. If the urge to move is uncontrollable and rain is not forthcoming, just soak both the area where the plant is presently growing and the hole you are moving it to. Dig the plant up and make the switch quickly, soaking the new site again. Mulch and water regularly until you see the plant perk up and start putting out new growth.

Step two: Continually add organic matter to improve your soil. You want soil to hold moisture, but you also want it to drain freely. I mulch with hay, which breaks down quickly and becomes part of the soil, especially in the heat of summer. Add compost whenever you plant and work it into intervening spaces.

Step three: Choose appropriate plants for your garden. Think in terms of plants native to your area as well as plants native to traditionally dry climates. Look at plants in your community that are thriving under less-than-optimal conditions.

In front of a local bank, surrounded by asphalt without a bit of shade all day, is a lush mound of gold and orange lantana that I never see being watered or pampered in any way. Now that is one tough plant, but everything a plant should be in terms of color, healthy foliage, and minimal care.

Step four: Limit turf areas. If I had my way, I would eliminate 95 percent of the lawn around my house. However, my husband thinks highly of turf (What is it about guys and grass?), so I just keep enlarging my mulched beds, eradicating grass inch by inch. I have a friend whose lawn takes three minutes to mow, but she has no husband so I guess that is a tradeoff.

Step five: Water deeply early in the morning (before 9 a.m.). You want the root systems of your plants to burrow into the ground rather than loll around in the top couple of inches of soil, which is what they will do if that is where the moisture is. It is much better to saturate the soil once a week than to wash off the foliage every day.

Step six: Mulch beds and borders with three to five inches of pinestraw, shredded bark, hay, leaves, or other organic materials. Mulching not only conserves moisture and keeps root systems cooler but the organic material also eventually enriches your soil, adding nutrients and moisture retention capability.

Xeriscaping used to be considered the wave of the future, but judging from the heat and minimal rainfall of the past couple of years I would call xeriscaping the wave of the present. Consider it a win-win-win-win process: Your garden will look better, you will work less, your water bill will decline, and you will be doing your bit for conservation. What a deal!

Consider the Lilies

"Consider the lilies," we are told for good reason. How lovely these flowers are in their simplicity and purity. Second only to roses, lilies have the longest history in horticulture and the most intriguing mystique. Lilies appear in frescos dated 1500 B.C., and an account of their origin is part of Greek mythology.

The goddess Hera was suckling the infant, Hercules, and when she fell asleep Hercules bit her, indicating it was high time for him to be weaned. Nevertheless, Hera's milk spilled; drops that fell on heaven became the Milky Way, and drops that spilled to earth became milk-white lilies.

Christians claimed the Madonna lily (*Lilium candidum*) as a symbol of chastity, a symbol of the easy life Adam and Eve enjoyed before their well-deserved expulsion from the Garden of Eden, and, of course, a symbol of the Virgin Mary herself.

Spring is an appropriate time for us to consider and to add to our gardens *Lilium longiflorum,* commonly called the Easter lily. This is the pot plant we fill our churches with on Easter Sunday and give to friends who invite us to Easter dinner.

Where do all these Easter lilies go? Why are our gardens not overflowing with them? I suspect that most of those foil-wrapped pots are tossed out within weeks of Easter. I have tossed a few myself, but vow to do better and, should someone give me a *L. longiflorum* for Easter, it will go into the garden where lilies belong.

The lily family includes almost 100 species, and hybridizers are hard at work developing increasingly vigorous, fragrant, floriferous, disease-resistant, and beautiful lilies, judging from the abundance I see and salivate over in bulb catalogs.

Lilies can be planted in spring or fall. Unlike daffodils, which are able to hang around unplanted for months, lily bulbs are never dormant so they should be planted when purchased, even if you put them in pots until you are ready to transfer them to your garden.

Dig a deep hole for your lily, incorporating compost to hold moisture. If your soil is heavy, place an inch or so of pebbles at the bottom of the hole to assure drainage. Except for the Madonna lily, which prefers alkaline soil, lilies thrive in slightly acidic soil. The bulb, a rounded clump of scales, should be placed (with roots spread out) so that its tip is at least three or four inches below the soil line.

Lilies form roots along the stem above the bulb, so planting the bulb deeply accomplishes two things: ample stem below the soil surface for roots to emerge and added stability for the stalk. If you plan to stake the lily, insert the stake at planting time so you can tie the stem as your lily grows. You will also be reserving that space for the lily, preventing yourself from planting something on top of it.

The earliest blooming lilies (besides Easter lilies raised in greenhouses) are Asiatic hybrids. An established clump of an Asiatic lily can bloom from early to mid-summer. The Asiatics are the hardiest and most reliable of the hybrids. Their stocky stems grow to about three feet so they need no staking, a definite plus.

In midsummer, Aurelian lilies bloom to the delight of hummingbirds who love them. The lily season ends with Oriental lilies, the most flamboyant and fragrant as well as the most susceptible to bulb rot and virus disease. Both Aurelians and Orientals grow to six feet, so they need to be staked or placed among plants that will hold them up.

While there are lilies native to North America and Europe, Asia is the horn of plenty for the lily family. Early in the nineteenth century, plant explorers hit the lily jackpot in China, Japan, Korea, and Tibet. For decades after, thousands of bulbs were shipped to the West. Many of these bulbs were susceptible to rot and viral diseases, but others proved hardy and most garden lilies are their descendents.

A favorite of mine is Formosa lily (*L. formosanum*), which was found in Taiwan in 1858 and brought to England in 1881. *L. formosanum* has clusters of fragrant white trumpet flowers, similar to those of the Easter lily. It grows six feet tall and blooms in late summer, which is why it is also called August lily.

Here is the magic part: The white trumpet blossom faces downward but, as it dries, it turns its face upward like golden candelabra.

I imagine that *L. formosanum* was something of a flop in England and anywhere north of New York. This lily not only enjoys the heat and humidity of Southern gardens, but it rots where summers are cool.

What I like most about *L. formosanum* is that it can be easily grown from seed and will bloom the same year if seeds are germinated early enough. Seeds are stored in the flower chambers, stacked like potato chips in tubes. Start seeds in fall, carry them through the winter, and plant the seedlings in the spring. You should have lilies galore by late summer. I have started seeds in early spring and still had blooms (albeit on twelve-inch stems) by September. The next year, the lilies were six feet tall.

When cutting blooms for arrangements or deadheading, remove just the top one-third to one-half of the stalk, leaving the rest to wither naturally.

I like lilies in the mixed border with their stalks surrounded (and supported) by other plants. Lilies, like clematis, are happiest when the soil at their feet is cool and shaded but their heads are basking in the sun.

The Dazzle of Daylilies

A friend, known in our community as "the daylily lady," visits on occasion and never fails to comment that my garden is nice but I do not have enough daylilies. Daylily people are like that. Obsessive. Passionate. Opinionated. Just like the rest of us.

What is it about gardeners that makes us fidgety in gardens that lack our personal favorites? I can hardly bear a garden without woods poppies. Or columbine. Or fothergilla. I like to think it is not bossiness that makes us this way but generosity, an eagerness to share the plants that please us most.

My friend is right about my garden. I do not have enough daylilies. But, then again, in a one-acre yard, I do not have sufficient space to have nearly enough of any plant.

For good reason, daylilies are regarded as the perfect perennial. Their foliage is handsome, their flowers exquisite. They are relatively carefree. They never wear out or tire of being divided. Their one fault is that they are addictive, especially for those with a yen to collect.

The daylily lady has more than 800 daylily cultivars in her garden, and she knows each one intimately. Her garden includes shrubs, perennials, annuals, trees, vines, groundcovers, and a water garden, but daylilies steal the show, especially in June.

Daylilies have a long season of bloom since hybridizers have developed early, midseason, and late bloomers. In my garden, daylilies are scattered around as cheerful residents of mixed borders and beds. This is how I like them best, surrounded by other flowers as if in a bouquet.

Daylilies prosper under almost any conditions. Some of mine are in partial shade, others in full sun. They grow in clay and they grow in sand. They bloom without complaint wherever they are planted, just as we all should do.

We have a house on a coastal island and I have a small garden there. Across the front of the house is a split rail fence, and ten years ago I planted daylilies on both sides of it. In sand and full sun, these daylilies have thrived. Here is the surprising part: Several times a year they are swamped by tidal floods that cover our yard. The tide recedes and the daylilies carry on as if nothing has happened.

If I were preparing a new border or bed of daylilies, I would put down a thick layer of newspapers on top of the grass or weeds, cover the papers with a truckload of compost, and then mulch the area. I would then let this space sit until the following fall or spring before planting daylilies or anything else.

But sometimes a gardener cannot wait months to plant. In this case, I would till the area (which is what we did around the split rail fence at the beach), adding compost to the soil. I would plant the daylilies, water well, and then mulch with newspaper and hay, pinestraw, shredded leaves, or dried seagrass.

Always select a mulching material that is plentiful, easily accessible, and cheap or free. That way you will never be tempted to skimp. With mulch, quantity is crucial.

When I decided to plant daylilies under the fence, I purchased twenty daylilies from the daylily lady who warned me to keep the plants labeled or they would be demoted to "seedlings" rather than "named" varieties. Of course I promptly mixed up the tags and am no longer sure who these guys are, which does not diminish my esteem for them. I do not have much of a pedigree myself.

I purchased other daylilies from a farmer who advertised them in my state's market bulletin, a rich source of inexpensive and unusual plants as well as hogs, horses, and tractor parts. The farmer had also lost track of his daylilies' tags though they too had once been named cultivars. That is why they were such a good buy.

Daylilies have names well worth remembering, such as Amazing Grace, Tahitian Falls, Raspberry Wine, Chorus Line, and Martha Edwards. Hybridizers get to name their babies and they do so with ingenuity and romantic flair.

When planting daylilies, dig a hole for each plant and mix in composted manure and dolomitic limestone. Hump the dirt in the middle of the hole so the plant sits at the same level it had been wherever it was growing before.

Set each plant on its hump with the roots spread out, scoop dirt over the roots, water well, and pull the mulch up around it. Plants should be spaced about two feet apart.

Daylilies' most important requirement is good drainage, making their survival of tidal floods even more surprising. They prefer slightly acid soil with high organic content, which top dressing and mulch should provide once the plants are established.

When I fertilize them, it is with fish emulsion. I wish I could say I apply it three times during the season to everything in my garden, including daylilies, but I cannot tell a lie (at least in print). Benign neglect is my mode of operation. However, most everything thrives and I am content.

Keeping daylilies groomed can be bothersome, but not if you inspect your garden frequently and do not have 800 cultivars. Snap off spent blooms that look like used tissues. Otherwise, daylilies go to seed, resulting in seedlings that may not be true to their mothers. Can you imagine?

A better way to make more daylilies is to divide crowded clumps into divisions of two "fans." I have separated daylilies with a hatchet, but, if you wash all the soil off, the rooted fans are pretty easy to pull apart. Daylilies should be divided every three years or so, when the number of blooms decreases or the roots feel wiggly because they are overcrowded.

I understand how daylily growers get hooked. First thing you know, backyard gardeners start hybridizing and the beat goes on: over-the-top color combinations, fancy double-ruffled petals, and the quest for white . . . or blue . . . or black. The search for new daylilies seems limitless. Personally, I am ready to leave well enough alone. Talk about gilding the lily! The daylilies in my garden have sufficient dazzle for me.

A Love-Hate Relationship with Iris

My attitude toward bearded iris comes close to a love-hate relationship. When the first blooms appear in May, I am overcome by desire. I want a dozen of every shade, fully realizing that bearded iris choices seem beyond count and ever changing. Iris hybridizers make sure of this and, as soon as an iris catalog is published, the list needs updating with breathtaking hybrids developed the previous week.

Bearded irises are, without question, stars of the early spring garden. Not only are they among the earliest bloomers, but they are also the most spectacular. For one thing, they are tall and stately, shooting upward in a burst of astonishing color and design. The flower itself has six segments. The upright segments (think of them as petals) are "standards," and the outer segments or petals are "falls." The beard is the furry strip running across the center of the fall.

Furthermore, the segments are flared, ruffled, crimped, or fringed and sometimes a combination of all four. Some are solid in color, and others fade from dark to light or contrast from starkest white to a purple that is almost black. No wonder people become addicted to bearded iris. There is something for everyone.

But we know that passion ebbs and love often ends in despair or boredom. Bearded iris can be a pain in the neck and other body parts, so a gardener has to come to grips eventually and ask herself if they are worth the effort. And, of course, the answer is no and yes.

Here is the basic problem for me: A bearded iris blooms for two amazing weeks in May and then sits around the rest of the year taking up space and not looking attractive at all. I try to think of iris foliage as spiky, an indispensable shape in the well-designed mixed border, but it is actually just gawky since, instead of standing upright the way spiky plants should, iris foliage leans to the left and to the right. Like me, it spreads outward rather than upward.

You can pull out or cut the sword-shaped foliage to six inches when it withers. If you are fussy, you can shape the leaves with scissors to your liking. Either way, bearded irises remain intrusive and you just have to ignore them or pull them up and plant them elsewhere, perhaps in your neighbor's garden.

Spring is as good a time as any to divide clumps of iris and plant new ones. Dig the clumps up and find a shady spot to sit. The rhizomes of bearded iris are easily divided. Discard sections of the rhizome that are soft or withered. Be sure each piece saved for replanting has a fan of leaves, and trim this fan to about six or eight inches so it is not top-heavy.

Irises are happiest in full sun but tolerate some shade. The planting site should be well drained, full of humus and dressed with rotted manure, bone meal, wood ashes, and other organic goodies. They will bloom without this tender loving care but do better when well nourished. Who doesn't?

Sometimes I think bearded irises should be planted in a separate bed that can look grand for a couple of weeks and ignored the rest of the year. Not many of us have enough space to do this or want to dedicate a whole section of good, humusy soil to a two-week extravaganza. Other times I think bearded irises do best planted here and there, like exclamation points, in a border that is interesting all year long.

When people complain to me that their irises do not bloom, I ask three questions: Do the irises get adequate sun? Can they see the tops of the rhizomes? Are the irises crowded? Irises need dividing approximately every three years. But the most likely problem is that the irises are planted too deeply. Like teenagers stretched out on a dock, iris rhizomes love the sun on their backs.

When planting iris, scoop out a shallow space, making a little bump in the center, and place the rhizome on the bump. Spread the roots out and cover with about an inch of soil. Then dust off the rhizome so its back is bared. Soak the ground and mulch lightly with hay or shredded leaves. The iris should bloom the following spring.

Like bearded iris, Japanese, Siberian, and crested irises grow from rhizomes, and their treatment is pretty much the same except that they require more water. Their foliage is less intrusive than that of bearded iris. In fact, their foliage is attractive and can be mistaken for ornamental grass.

My own hands-down favorite iris, however, is the Dutch iris and I cannot figure out why everyone does not plant them. Dutch iris grow from bulbs, and you can buy a hundred or more for the price of a fancy bearded iris.

Dutch iris blooms are smaller than bearded iris but they are elegant. Next to a Dutch iris, a bearded iris looks excessive. Tarty, even. A single Dutch iris bloom lasts a week, not a day, and the foliage is like daffodil foliage. A month or two after the Dutch iris blooms, the foliage obligingly withers away until the following spring when it emerges.

Dutch iris come in blue, yellow, bronze, and white, a refreshing simplicity compared to the bearded iris panorama. You probably will have to buy your own Dutch iris. While folks are always giving away bearded iris rhizomes, we tend to hang on to Dutch iris bulbs because we never have too many. Regrettably, Dutch iris bulbs do not have the long life span bearded iris rhizomes do. Now that is something for hybridizers to work on.

I certainly hope I have not stepped on any toes (or rhizomes) when it comes to bearded iris. If you are infatuated, I have been there and could not have been dissuaded from blowing the grocery money on a 'Beverly Sills' when she was new. Gardening is a hobby of visceral passion and strong opinions that change with the seasons, and I would not have it any other way.

A Love-Hate Relationship with Iris

Gardening with the Enemy

"We have a mole," my walking buddy complains. "Voles have eaten my seedlings," wails a fellow Master Gardener. "Deer are chomping on my azaleas," chimes in a desperate reader. Pests abound and normally gentle gardeners are angry enough to bring out the poisons, guns, traps, and whatever it takes to rid them of their enemies.

I was so disturbed by the moans and threats of my fellow gardeners that I traveled to England to see what the Brits were doing in the way of garden protection. After all, they have a long history of maintaining gardens that are the envy of American horticulturists.

At Wisley, the Royal Horticultural Society's crown jewel of a garden southwest of London, I purchased a book called *Common Garden Enemies* by Janet Thompson. Thompson had previously published a book called *Gardening with the Enemy: A Guide to Rabbit-Proof Gardening*. The preposition "with" bespoke an amiable approach that appeals to me more than the poisons and guns my friends are waving.

Thompson describes moles as furry little snout-nosed creatures who consume insect larvae (grubs) and earthworms and burrow across lawns to find these delicacies. It is the tunnels that seem to bother people, although my walking buddy was concerned about her earthworms. That I can understand.

I do not find the tunnels unsightly, but I am not a lawn person. The lawn is just something to walk across to get to the borders as far as I am concerned. Actually, I kind of like the feel of a soft tunnel under my feet and the overnight appearance of elongated bumps.

A few years ago, when mole tunnels appeared in our lawn, I mentioned them to my husband warily since he is not as organically inclined as I am. I was pleased with his response, however, when he said, "Think of them as aerating the soil." And that was that. The moles moved on (I like to think they ran out of grubs and lost their appetite for earthworms), and I have not been bothered by them again.

The author of *Common Garden Enemies* has several suggestions for seriously discouraging moles. Buy something called Mole Smokes that, when lit, permeate the tunnels with sulphurous gas; or wrap crushed garlic cloves in muslin and drop them into the runs; or, smellier yet, soak a rag with creosote and stick that into the tunnel.

Another suggestion is to put mothballs and burnt pepper in the tunnel. Evidently moles' snouts are sensitive to noxious odors. How about this bit of advice? Drop a slice of rancid fish into the burrow.

If herbal remedies are your cup of tea, place some elder twigs or sticks of rhubarb into the molehill, or plant a lot of caper spurge (*Euphorbia lactea*) where moles congregate. Moles must be as sensitive to sound as they are to odors since one remedy is to bury a bottle in the garden next to the tunnel so the bottle top is level with the soil surface. Moles will move away from the sound of the wind blowing across the top, that is, assuming the wind blows.

Or stick a purchased battery-operated stake into the ground. Its deep sound reputedly scares off ground rodents within 850 square yards. I suspect this remedy solves the problem by persuading the moles to move to your neighbors' yards. This can be touchy, but it works. A friend of mine put little vibrating windmills around her property and her moles moved on, she knows not where and is not asking.

As for voles, who inhabit tunnels left behind by vacating moles, you can poison or trap them as you would a mouse in the attic. You can fill your garden with gravel, eight inches or so deep, and that might move them on to your neighbors. Or you can get a cat . . . preferably a hungry cat with a brother or two.

A remedy Thompson fails to mention in *Common Garden Enemies* is dowsing the ground with urine. Host a party, serve plenty of beer, and encourage the gentlemen to browse around the outside perimeter of the garden. I cannot vouch for the method but I read about using urine for this purpose years ago in *House and Garden* magazine, so it must be true.

As for deer, since I live on a suburban street surrounded by other suburban streets, I do not share the distress of my more wooded friends. Thompson, however, deals with the problem emphatically since deer annoy British gardeners at least as much as they do Americans.

Here is my favorite suggestion: Spread lion dung around the periphery of the garden. If you do not have a lion handy, you can evidently purchase clay pellets impregnated with liquidized dung.

Thompson thinks North American gardeners might prefer a variation: coyote urine.

Other suggestions are to wrap trees with plastic guards or wire mesh, purchase deer scaring devices, set up trip wires, erect an electric fence, or toss rotten eggs around the property. Doesn't that sound like a pleasant pastime?

The most effective way to beat deer at the nibbling game is to rely on plants that do not whet their appetites. Deer avoid foliage with scratchy coarse textures, and who can blame them? Bristled yucca, sandpaper-textured pulmonaria, stiff eulalia grass, and fuzzy-leafed joe pye weed come to mind. County extension offices, garden magazines, and the Internet offer lists of plants that deer supposedly snub, although no plant seems foolproof when a hungry buck is on the prowl.

Lists of deer-proof plants may limit your plant selection to an unbearable point if, like me, you long for at least one of everything. I suggest you do what my friend who lives in harmony with nature, at the edge of the woods, did for her horticultural peace of mind.

In most of her large wooded garden, she concentrates on plants deer eschew (that is, they choose not to chew), but she has enclosed an area next to the house with black mesh fencing material over seven feet tall. Because of her garden design, you do not even notice the fencing unless you look for it.

In this enclosed area, she has planted an assortment of shrubs, perennials, herbs, bulbs, and annuals that might be too tempting to a hungry buck. At the front and the back she has had wooden fencing and gates built so the area is actually a walled garden, full of her favorites that remain safe from nibbling deer. So far.

We have to remember that *we* are the invaders. We remove habitats and create irresistible meccas as we build our houses and grow our gardens. I suggest we take an oath to indeed work "with" the so-called enemies . . . unless, of course, we are talking about slugs. Where is that poison? Get the gun!

I'll Never Be a Bedder

In the twenty years or so that I have been gardening, I have gone through obsessive and passionate phases, all of which have been instructive and satisfying.

I have been an herb gardener, a mixed-border gardener, and, most recently, a wildlife gardener. In fact, I still am all three. One type of gardener I have never been and will never be, however, is a bedder.

A "bedder" is a gardener who selects a particular plant and perhaps even a specific color of that plant. Then he or she puts in large groups or beds of purple petunias or red salvias or whatever the plant of choice happens to be.

Far be it from me to condemn bedders. Every gardener to her own obsession. But I cannot help feeling pity for these folks (unless they own motels or gas stations or oversee public works) who are missing the excitement of planting a little of this, a little of that, making every garden stroll an adventure.

Perennials are not usually cultivated in these large beds because of their cost and shorter bloom period. It is the annual that is favored by these johnny-one-notes of the gardening world. Annuals are inexpensive enough to plant in masses, have long bloom periods if deadheaded, and are reliable. Plant a six-pack of marigolds in April and you pretty much know how they will look in July.

I like a variety of annuals mixed in among herbs, perennials, and shrubs. Even if it is a mass of gorgeous color, a choice of one is not for me when I can have a smorgasbord.

The hardest task is limiting my choices among annuals to ten or twelve or twenty. My pocketbook does this for me. But, if I can choose just ten, I would probably buy a six-pack or two of all the following annuals, basing my selection on color, height, and ability to withstand the vicissitudes of a hot Southern summer.

My first choice is globe amaranth, or gomphrena. This is a plant about sixteen or twenty inches tall that blooms enthusiastically no matter what summertime inflicts. The one-inch clover-like blooms are magenta, rose, or white and can be admired in the garden, used as cut flowers, or dried for wreaths and winter arrangements.

Or perhaps zinnias would be my first choice, as well as my second through fifth, since I plant several kinds. Zinnias come in a treasure trove of sizes and colors, and I admire them all. My first pick is *Zinnia angustifolia*, which is eight to ten inches tall and spreads about twenty inches, a great front-of-the-border bloomer. It comes in orange, gold, and white.

Of course, I also love the tall zinnias with six-inch ruffled blooms and the midsized single zinnias that are the favorite landing pads of butterflies.

Melampodium is a shrubby annual about eighteen inches tall. Like *Z. angustifolia*, it is covered with small daisy-like blooms and hangs in there from early summer until hard frost. The flowers are gold, and the foliage is muted kelly green.

There is nothing muted about tithonia, or Mexican sunflower, another butterfly magnet. The scarlet-orange, yellow-centered flowers are stunning. "Wow!" is the usual reaction from first-time viewers. In a wet summer, tithonia will grow eight feet tall, but five or six feet is more usual, as well as more manageable.

Rather than massing them in a group, since they are such attention grabbers, I plant single tithonias in different areas of the yard, wherever I have space and want to make a sculptural statement. A couple of them usually flop over in a summer storm. I just leave them prone and, in a week or two, the stems turn the corner, start heading skyward, and continue to bloom

Two annual vines I could not forego are cypress vine (*Ipomoea purpurea*) and my recent discovery, exotic love (*Mina lobata*). Cypress vine has red tubular flowers, the delight of hummingbirds, and exotic love has late-blooming yellow and orange flowers. I do not know why it is called exotic love, but the name is definitely catchy.

Salvia coccinea 'Lady in Red' is a red-hot annual that starts blooming in late summer and continues into the fall. It is a sturdy two-foottall bushy plant that hummingbirds and butterflies flock to, making it a necessity in my garden. Another annual salvia I enjoy is *S. c.* 'Snow Nymph,' which is white and subdues my usually overheated borders. Both reseed themselves, and I appreciate that.

To my delight, cosmos is the most common wildflower-of-choice on highways I travel. This should tell us something about its vitality.

Butterflies love cosmos, especially the yellow sulphur varieties. While cosmos grows as tall as four to five feet, the shorter two-foot-tall dwarfs work better in my garden.

However, a tall annual that does hold its own in my garden is cleome, which blooms from early summer until the first real frost. Cleomes are definitely drought-tolerant and tough, though their spidery blooms appear airy and delicate. Some people dislike their smell, but I am not offended by it. Nor am I offended when it reseeds itself. An acquaintance with a fabulous vegetable garden always grows cleomes among her cabbage plants. It seems cabbage loopers prefer the flowers to the vegetable. Probably that aroma.

That is the pared-down list of favorite heat- and drought-tolerant annuals, and I have not even gotten to marigolds, pentas, or coleus.

In my garden, annuals are never planted in groups larger than three to five, although groupings are repeated in multiple locations. I think half the fun is discovering where plants do best and what combinations make my gardener's heart sing.

However you plant annuals, in small groups like mine or in beds of thousands, your garden will be enriched, not only by their color but also by their vitality and resilience, inspirations to us all.

I'll Never Be a Bedder

Turf Battles

Over forty years as a householder have taught me the following about grass: It always needs to be mowed when you want to do something else.

Grass is a magnet for critters such as mole crickets, grubs, aphids, and fire ants. No matter what the gardener does, it is regularly invaded by weeds with names like knotwood, Florida betony, goosegrass, prostrate spurge, and nutsedge. Furthermore, it is attacked by blights such as red thread, brown patch, dollar spot, and something called fairy ring.

This onslaught of bugs and fungi should not surprise us since grass, pampered and petted in lawn after lawn (not to mention golf course after golf course), is America's most blatant example of monoculture. Planting a single crop over large areas invites insect infestations, fungi, and diseases. Remember cotton? Tobacco? Boll weevils? Tobacco mosaic?

Agri-industrialists have become zillionaires through the production of herbicides, insecticides, and fungicides to be poured onto our lawns and, inevitably, filtered into our ground water.

I read recently that Americans mow 31 million acres of lawn every year, using 300 million gallons of gas as well as 1 billion hours that could be spent playing tennis, fishing, or reading books. We lawn owners spend $17.4 billion a year on everything from 70 million pounds of pesticides to gas-guzzling lawn tractors. Notice this figure does not include the cost of labor, either our own or that of a lawn management company.

Furthermore, we all know people who have cut down perfectly beautiful and useful shade trees so grass would grow.

Where did this love affair with (or mania for) lawns begin? The earliest settlers sensibly planted vegetables and useful herbs around their cabins, adding perhaps a shrub or two for looks and a few flowers for pleasure.

Now we devote hours of effort and billions of dollars to grow a crop we cannot eat, be cured by, or sell. Our goal seems to be to produce something that looks as uninteresting as indoor-outdoor carpet but needs perpetual care.

I do know why the Rochesters have a lawn. It is because everyone on our street has one. That, I suspect, is the reason most people have lawns and may account for the history of lawns. One lord of the manor ordered his serfs to scythe the front pasture and all the neighboring lords followed suit like sheep.

However, times may be changing. Not long ago, I read a column in *Horticulture* by garden designer Jenks Farmer about his Columbia, South Carolina, lawn of unmowed, unfettered zoysia grass. I have seen zoysia grown this way and it is beautiful, moving in the breeze and producing varied texture and color unlike crew-cut grass that just sits there, static and kelly green.

My own favorite turf area is a twenty-foot-long oval in the middle of my mixed border. It used to be a boring patch of centipede sod but, because groundcovers and reseeding annuals creep outward from the border, the lawn has become a tapestry of colors and textures. My first inclination was to pull out uninvited guests but then I realized how pleasing the mix is, at least to me. No doubt a grass purist would curl his lip, but what do I care?

Not long ago, organic gardening and groceries were off the beaten track, somewhere on the lunatic fringe. Now organic strategies are the first line of defense for knowledgeable gardeners. Organic foods are taking over an increasing amount of shelf space in supermarkets. Even Burger King sells vegetarian burgers. Can the abandonment of high-maintenance, water-consuming lawns be far behind?

In the seventies, Lorrie Otto founded the Wild Ones organization in Milwaukee, urging homeowners to let lawns go natural and to garden with native plants. Wild Ones chapters are popping up around the country, wherever gardeners are coming to their senses.

About the time the Wild Ones were organizing, native plant enthusiasts were regarded as eccentric. Now sophisticated homeowners are replacing lawns with native grasses with alluring names such as prairie dropseed, royal catchfly, prairie smoke, and meadow blazing star. More and more, homeowners want to create (or recreate) natural wildlife habitats and to get the chemicals out of their yards.

A posh planned community in Florida forbids homeowners from planting lawn grass because it is not a native plant. A New England town awards prizes to citizens who vary their landscapes, replacing grass with more eco-friendly plantings.

A Southwestern water authority gives "water hero" awards to businesses that install xeriscapes rather than traditional lawns. Homeowners in an Arizona community get rebates for purchasing drought-tolerant shrubs.

The best news is that individual homeowners who dare to be different are winning in court when neighborhood associations sue them for returning their lawns to a more natural state.

Always the optimist, on the lookout for ecological progress, I am happy to report a rapidly expanding number of yards in my own suburban neighborhood with decreased grassy areas and mulched islands of trees and shrubs. Even better, I see yards in very expensive developments with almost no grass at all, only naturalized swaths of shrubs and groundcovers.

I have to admit that I have not seen examples of let-it-go meadows in the city or suburbs, but I keep hoping.

I look longingly at fields of native grasses, admiring their diversity and mobility. Am I ready to turn my own boring lawn into a sea of grass? Not likely. But it sure would be grand to live on a street where we all agreed to turn in our mowers and let nature take her course.

The Show Goes On

Not long ago I dropped by to visit a friend's garden and was puzzled when she insisted I come inside. We walked around the rooms of her house and, from six strategic windows, she did indeed show me her garden.

From each window, I could see an attractive border (or vignette) in the space visible from the house. As we looked out the dining room window, we saw flowering shrubs, a couple of small trees, ferns, groundcovers, and perennials. Outside the kitchen window was a fenced vegetable and herb garden. From the bedroom, we viewed a natural area of trees and understory shrubs.

I was charmed. Never had I considered garden design from the viewpoint of the house. To be honest, I rarely think about garden design at all. My borders happen haphazardly as I add space and install plants in what I hope are appropriate places.

However, I have in fact created one "vista" of sorts outside French doors that lead from our family room to the yard. Forty years ago, long before I became a gardener, I staked out the chair next to these doors as my territory. I have always liked looking outwards.

Once I became a gardener, I began developing this space, catering to my interest in wildlife as well as to my passion for color. As a result, throughout the year, I am treated to a continual show of flora and fauna that never fails to enchant me. The border is no more than six by twelve feet, about the size of some walk-in closets, but the action in this arena is nonstop.

A large butterfly bush (*Buddleia davidii* 'White Profusion') trimmed into a tree form is the star of the show. Unable to leave well enough alone, last year I planted a red cypress vine below the butterfly bush so the vine twined upward through the branches. Hummingbirds heartily approved the combination.

The problem was that a butterfly bush needs continual deadheading to remove spent flowers. If I deadheaded, I cut off the vine along with the dead flowers. If I did not deadhead, the butterfly bush would stop blooming and I would be stuck with an ugly brown shrub in center stage.

I cut off dead blooms as best I could, unwrapping the vine or cutting it back. I considered cutting down the butterfly bush but, when I showed up with a saw, two Swallowtails dropped by, reminding me why I had planted it.

This year I planted the cypress vine on azaleas lined up in back of this border. They could use perking up and, unlike the butterfly bush, they have nothing to do all summer but hang around, taking up space.

I have nine butterfly bushes in my yard: five whites, a pink, two blues, and a purple. I abide by that revered gardening maxim: Too much is not nearly enough. Deadheading continues to be a nuisance, but the tradeoff in butterflies, hummingbirds, and bees makes it worth the effort.

Two of the whites I trim as trees, giving me room to plant underneath and adding height to the borders. All five white butterfly bushes came from the same parent plant, a passalong from a friend I am reminded of with every bloom.

The pink is *Buddleia* 'Pink Delight,' and it too is a passalong given to me by a friend who abhors any butterfly bush that is not pink. When I planted all those whites I thought that butterflies were most attracted to white, but I have read since that they, like my friend, prefer pink.

The purple is huge and out of control, although I cut all my butterfly bushes to the ground (and butterfly trees to the trunk) late in February. By the end of June, this one is seven feet tall and six feet wide.

The least weedy butterfly bushes are the blues, *Buddleia* 'Lochinch,' which are more lavender than blue, but I forgive them since they have year-round matte gray foliage.

But back to the border I see from my chair. In back of the butterfly tree are joe pye weeds (*Eupatorium purpureum* 'Gateway'). It takes about three years to get joe pye moving, but he is worth the wait. The dusty pink blooms are butterfly favorites.

Under and around the butterfly bush is a mass of royal blue *Salvia guaranitica,* so enticing that you can stand right next to a stalk and a hummingbird will hover within a foot of you as it sips. I also grow the annual salvia, 'Lady in Red' and Mexican bush sage. Something indeed for everyone and too much for those who like nature subdued.

Also in this border is *Lantana camara* 'Miss Huff.' I love plants with people's names. You know a story lurks. A birdbath and a bird feeder provide sustenance for feathered friends, and a flat dish of muddy water sits on the ground for the butterflies.

Tucked in front of the shrubs are as many perennials and annuals as I can cram in: blue *Baptisia australis*, purple coneflower, *Sedum* 'Autumn Joy,' and bright orange butterfly weed (*Asclepias tuberosa*). Herbs that add texture and fragrance include fennel, rue, lemon marigold (*Tagetes lemonii*), Thai basil, parsley, and ornamental *Oregano* 'Herrenhausen.' The herbs also tone down the color palette, which is a good thing since I am not going to do it myself.

Dwarf coreopsis edges the front, and goldenrod (*Solidago* 'Golden Fleece') creeps outward late in the summer. An ever-increasing crop of four-foot-tall purple Mexican petunias (*Ruellia brittoniana*) rise above the fray, and *Cassia corymbosa* produces a cloud of yellow blossoms by late summer. Daffodils, daylilies, and lilies appear when the time is right.

This border is crowded with color, texture, scents, and, most of all, life. Whatever effort this small garden takes is meager compared to the pleasure given by the creatures who linger here. No matter what season it is or which creature is on stage, the show continues and is a performance that never palls.

The Siren Sound of Water

I had steeled myself against the gathering mania for water gardening and thought I had eluded it in this lifetime.

For years, I just said "No" to ponds and waterfalls. I have never been drawn to relationships with fish, having sufficient daily interaction with a Labrador retriever and a schnauzer. Nor do I care much for plants that grow in water. Contact with the soil is essential to my gardening experience.

As I was prowling around a friend's yard recently, thinking she was not at home, I heard the barely audible sound of moving water. I looked around and nowhere did I see the source of this music. No satyr or cupid spouting water from its mouth or nether parts. No tiered fountain dribbling water into a clam-shaped basin.

At last I discovered the origin of that siren sound, and it was then that I fell in love. In the corner of my friend's mixed border was a glazed pottery urn, standing waist-high and topped off by a sheet of water that moved like silk over the rim and down the sides of the urn. No splash, no gurgle, no fountain plume . . . just the soft sound of water sliding across the top of the container and down its surface.

Passion soared. I felt the pangs of envy. "Water gardening" took on new meaning, and I had to have an urn of my own.

As I stared covetously, my friend emerged from her house looking surprised to find a stalker in her midst. Fortunately she is good-natured and generous and she knew the urn was too heavy for me to filch, at least without a couple of muscular assistants.

Not only is this urn (and its hypnotic sound) wondrous to see and hear, it is also, according to my friend, trouble-free. Although hers was installed by a professional, she assured me that all I would need is electricity, a pot or urn, a pump, a basin, and some rocks and no effort on my part, once it is up and running.

The basin goes in the ground, and the pump goes in the basin. The little hose from the pump goes through the hole in the bottom of whatever container is being used. Of course, I want a waist-high urn just like my friend's. A layer of rocks encircles the urn and covers the basin and pump.

The water skims across the top of the urn, down the sides, into the basin where it is pumped back into the urn. Fish and plants are not a part of the mix so there is nothing to feed, plant, or divide, though thirsty birds are invited guests.

At a nearby public botanical garden, smaller and subtler containers are placed throughout the borders and islands. You hear them before you see them, and the sound adds immeasurably to the garden tour. After all, isn't sensory delight what gardens are all about? A feast for the eyes, the nose, and, now, the ears.

Then I fell in love again, this time with a gnarled stump and a metal bucket in another friend's garden. Still no lilies, no koi, no spouting elf or frog. This friend took an ordinary galvanized bucket, added a clever husband, and made a water feature with a flowing spigot that never stops or overflows.

For this project, you need (in addition to the bucket and maybe the husband) a piece of pipe four to six inches longer than the depth of the bucket, a faucet, half-inch plastic tubing, and a small recirculating pump.

Attach the tubing to the pump. Attach the faucet to the pipe. Run the tubing through the pipe to the faucet. Place the pipe in the bucket, stabilizing it against the interior wall. Fill the bucket at least half full of water to cover the pump completely. Plug the pump's cord into an outlet and let the music begin. Keep the water level near the top of the bucket if you want birds to be part of the entertainment.

The same friend and her clever husband dug a large gnarled stump out of a field to create a water feature delightful to eyes and ears. They drilled several holes up and through the stump and inserted plastic tubing from the pump into the stump.

In a waterproof basin sunk into the ground, they placed the pump with the stump on top. The container was filled with water. When the pump is plugged in, the water bubbles out of the stump and over the meandering surfaces.

To add to the magic, they placed large rocks over the edge of the basin to hide the mechanism and added grasses and other plants to make the stump look as if it had been in their garden for years. Birds and squirrels drop by to sip and preen.

The Siren Sound of Water

Is there one more obsession on the horizon? I visited another friend whose garden includes a fishpond. Ho hum. But then I spotted a turtle catching a snooze and a lizard sunning herself on a rock. At the edge, a dozen tadpoles frolicked, frogs in the making. "Be still my heart," I said sternly.

I stopped on my way home to browse around the garden center. Liners and pumps were on sale.

❧

144

CHAPTER 5

Summer

This is the season of abundance. Plants intertwine and mesh
so it is sometimes hard to know where one stops and
another begins. That is the way I like it.

Summer Shrubs on the Shy Side

Some things in life are just so downright dependable they provide stability and comfort in a world often plagued by unexpected events and turmoil. Take, for instance, the shrubs of summer, unassuming plants that hang around shyly until they suddenly burst into bloom when you have forgotten they are there.

As I strolled around my garden, head downward, checking for evidence of nibbling slugs, something pink caught my eye just as a spicy-sweet fragrance captured my nose. In the middle of the shady island under a large hickory tree, I was face to face with the perfectly named "summersweet."

Summersweet (or sweet pepperbush) is actually *Clethra alnifolia*, and I have two: 'Ruby Spice' in the shady island and a white-spiked dwarf variety, 'Hummingbird,' in a semicircular border against the house. The attention-grabbing blooms on both are four- to six-inch bottlebrushes at the tip of almost every branch. The scent is far reaching though not cloying, alluring to bees as well as to discriminating people.

Summersweet prefers moist, acidic soil and shade but will tolerate dryness and even full sun. This is a woodland plant, a Southeastern native, which accounts for its toughness. The native clethra grows to ten feet but the named varieties reach just four to eight feet, and 'Hummingbird' is three to four feet. While clethra needs no pruning, it can be cut to the ground at the end of winter. I have never done this, but I do remove the oldest stems to keep it shapely.

In the fall, the blooms morph into grayish round seedpods that hang on through winter. I always welcome something to look at in January. While clethra spreads by suckers along creek banks and in wet ditches, I have never found it invasive in my garden.

Another woodland native, *Calycanthus floridus*, is a different story and suckers enthusiastically into a thicket. Traditionally known as sweet shrub or Carolina allspice, it has handsome glossy green, textured foliage but its major attraction is its scent. Everything about calycanthus is aromatic: the unassuming brownish-red flowers, the leaves, the roots, and the bark.

Calycanthus was the first plant that went into my woodland garden. Except for pulling up suckers that appear up to six feet away from the mother plant and removing seed pods that look like big dried figs, I pay it scant attention until I catch a whiff of that scent that will not leave a gardener alone. In the fall, those shiny green leaves turn gold.

Another summer favorite is bush clover or *Lespedeza thunbergii*, which enjoys full sun but tolerates part shade. When I point out this six-foot shrub to visitors, they often say something like "I thought lespedeza was a weed." Well, some are, some aren't. This genus includes about 150 species, and I cannot vouch for all of them.

The one in my mixed border is 'White Fountain,' which gives you an image of how it looks in full bloom. The bluish-green leaves are about an inch long and rounded . . . a pretty plain-jane plant until it covers itself with thousands of white pea-like flowers. Then in the fall, and this may be the best part, the foliage becomes bright yellow.

Lespedeza comes in several white forms as well as rosy pink. I saw a dwarf variety at a local nursery and made the mistake of not buying it. I will not let that happen again.

I treat lespedeza like other summer bloomers such as buddleia and lantana, letting it sit out the winter with little or no pruning back. Then I cut it to the ground in late winter.

Lespedeza is an easy plant to love with no pests, no diseases, and late summer blooms, just when a gardener needs them most. I have enjoyed 'White Fountain' in my mixed border so much that I now have one in my woodland garden and in a shady shrub bed facing the street. When I locate those dwarfs, they too will have space in the mixed border.

We tend to think of spireas as spring bloomers, but *Spirea xbumalda* 'Goldflame' and 'Anthony Waterer' will bloom all summer and until frost if the flowers are clipped off. Both shrubs thrive in full sun to part shade.

'Goldflame' has chartreuse foliage with pink flowers, admittedly an odd combination but who am I to argue with Mother Nature? When the foliage first appears, it has a russet tinge, then it turns yellow and remains chartreuse the rest of the summer. I use these mounding three-foot shrubs among foundation plants in the front of the house and as specimen plants in the mixed borders.

147

Summer Shrubs on the Shy Side

'Anthony Waterer' has less interesting green foliage and magenta flowers. It flourishes as a specimen plant in the partially shaded front garden and in the sunny mixed border.

Evidence abounds that a gardener never stops growing. Early this summer I discovered another flowering shrub, indigofera, which I suspect we will all be hearing more of soon. Upon the enthusiastic recommendation of a well-known plantsman, I purchased *Indigofera amblyantha* or "tall indigo," which will reach eight feet and flower from April to mid-October. This is another shrub to cut to the ground in late winter.

Indigofera spreads by rhizomes, which does not scare me at all since I am smitten. "Too much is not nearly enough" is one of my guiding principles. Indigofera appears in a variety of forms, from my tree-tall specimen down to three-foot spreaders. Their common trait is the wisteria-like little pink flowers that form racemes of four to five inches.

A serious mistake made by many gardeners is overattention to spring, forgetting the bounty of other seasons. Summer shrubs may not have the flamboyance of azaleas, but they also do not have lace bugs, aphids, or chlorosis. Furthermore, they do not give up when the heat is on. And neither should we.

A Rule of Green Thumb: Prune after Bloom

One of my favorite books is *The Well-Tended Perennial Garden* by Tracy DiSabato-Aust. I tip my garden hat to DiSabato-Aust every time I make the rounds of my mixed border with hedge clippers and whack off a dozen deadheads with one fell swoop.

Thanks to her, gone are the tedious hours of clipping off spent daisies or veronica or salvia one at a time. I now pick out an appropriate level and, with my hedge clippers, cut the plant back to that point. Admittedly, the plant looks chopped (which is not surprising) but, in a week or two, it is lush and verdant and improved by the experience.

This is a fact of life. If you want your garden to look good through summer and fall, you absolutely must deadhead. A plant blooms to produce seed. By removing spent flowers (which are seedheads), you encourage the plant to try again.

This is especially true of annuals, but also true of many perennials. In fact, some trees, such as crepe myrtles and vitex, will rebloom if you remove seedheads. Even without rebloom, the foliage looks better and the plant is more robust and shapely as a result of being cut back.

Here is the basic rule: Prune after bloom. Of course, the rule can be broken and sometimes should be. You might prune to delay bloom or to promote larger blooms. Or prune very tall plants (such as tithonia and swamp sunflower) in July to control height so they do not fall over later in the season. Or prune to stagger heights of plants so all your daisies are not thirty inches tall.

If you are the controlling type, you can cut back plants to keep them in their own space. Since I am happily out of control in my garden, my plants intertwine and mesh, so it is sometimes hard to know where one stops and another begins. That is the way I like it.

However, sometimes, even for me, too much is too much. The other day I was checking out the public garden I tend and realized that three small conifers were completely covered by chartreuse sweet potato vine (*Ipomoea batatas* 'Margarita'). I took out my pocketknife and cut the vines back, giving those poor blue junipers sunlight and fresh air. I know they felt better and I did too, and 'Margarita' will get over it in time.

Cutting back or pruning helps control pests by providing air circulation and removing damaged foliage. When not overdone, pruning improves the overall appearance of your garden and may give you that smug feeling exemplary housekeepers get from spring cleaning. Not that I have any personal experience in this regard.

But here is the best part of all: Working your way around your garden enables you to bond with your plants. Think of the renovation you are doing as a form of meditation. You renew not only your borders but also your spirit, which is a good thing because, in the zone where I garden, we have another four or five months of good gardening weather to enjoy.

Making decisions about the best cutting-back place may be tricky, but think of it this way. The plant will regrow no matter what mistake you make. I have always wondered why women (and an increasing number of men) bewail a bad haircut. It is hair; it will grow back to be cut again . . . and again and again. Plants are the same. If you cut them back too far or they look scalped, time will take care of the problem.

Observe where new growth is already taking place. For instance, some plants (such as feverfew and artemisia) start sprouting new foliage at ground level. I prune back to that. Some plants sprout foliage at the base of flowering stems. I cut them there, hoping new stems will emerge and bloom.

I pick a cool day or the coolest part of a hot day and work my way around the mixed border. I carry a basket that holds my pruners, hedge clippers, and trowel.

I work best on my knees, so I tote one of those kneelers with side handles that helps me get up off the ground. I treated myself to a kneeler when I found myself crawling over to a tree or a bench to get myself back to standing position. I figure this gadget will keep me gardening into my nineties, as long as my arms hold out.

With my tools and kneeler, I work my way around the borders pulling up strays, whacking deadheads and rangy stems, and digging up sideshoots of perennials to be potted up. I pull out plants that are not doing their jobs, and occasionally I move perennials that are mis-placed.

I do not recommend transplanting at this time of the year, but sometimes a gardener does what a gardener has to do. For instance, last spring I planted some red-striped sorrel that was supposed to grow three feet tall. They never got taller than twelve inches, so this morning I moved them from midborder where they were swallowed to the front where they could be admired.

DiSabato-Aust is not the only author who has changed my gar-dening life, but I never pick up hedge clippers without thinking about her, just as I never look at my garden without thinking of the people who have given me plants . . . or cuttings . . . or seeds. Garden writers and gardeners alike pass along what we have learned and what we love, little enough to give in return for what we have been given.

A Rule of Green Thumb: Prune after Bloom

Tomatoes Are for Everyone, Almost

I am trying to recall individuals I have encountered in my lifetime who do not like tomatoes fresh from the garden. I can think of three: One of them is my oldest son who began rebelling at the age of four by extracting tomato bits from his salad and turning up his little nose at a proffered BLT. The other two individuals have disappeared into oblivion, possibly as a result of scurvy.

If I had to choose between growing flowers and growing tomatoes, I might opt for tomatoes. Fortunately I do not have to decide and can have it all, exactly what I deserve, at least garden-wise. As I stand over the sink, taking a bite from the first tomato sandwich of summer, I am reminded how blessed I am.

Every year I plant a main crop of modern hybrids such as Park's Whopper, Celebrity, or Better Boy, all disease-resistant varieties suitable for our area's climate. I know they are disease-resistant because they are labeled VFN, meaning they are tough customers when it comes to verticillium wilt, fusarium wilt, and nematodes.

In addition, I always plant one or two heirloom tomatoes out of principle. I have planted Mortgage Lifter and Brandywine in the past, but this year I am trying German Johnson, which was recommended to me by a friend who, in exchange for a gorgeous view of a large lake, gardens in hard red clay. We will see how they do in my sand.

Last fall I moved my tomato garden from one side of our acre lot to the other. I covered a grassy area with about eight sheets of newspaper, covered the paper with compost, and covered the compost with approximately eight inches of hay. I distributed pelleted lime over the area and let this sandwich sit quietly, waiting for spring.

I moved my tomato plot not for the sake of horticultural hygiene but because I wanted a woodland garden where tomatoes have been growing the past ten years. I should have moved them years ago to avoid nematode infestation but, like most gardeners with limited initiative and space, I depended upon the presence of sunlight and continually improved soil to compensate for laziness and cramped quarters.

Because I cannot rotate my tomato location every three years, I probably will always have my share of nematodes. I do interplant garlic chives and southernwood, two herbs reputed to discourage nematodes. I have no empirical data regarding their success, but we always have enough BLTs and sliced tomatoes to suit us. Evidence enough for me.

Though I have seen a few tomato hornworms in my gardening life (and disposed of them by handpicking and squishing with an emphatic stomp of my garden clogs), aphids and spider mites do not hang around my tomato patch. A miracle happens after gardening organically for a few years. Well-nourished soil produces healthier plants, which are less attractive to destructive insects.

Furthermore, good guys take care of bad guys. Justice prevails. I encourage beneficial insects by planting dill and fennel for lacewings, and Queen Anne's lace, tansy, spearmint, and zinnias for lady beetles. If aphids or spider mites did appear, I would spray them off the plant with the hose or an organic insecticidal soap.

When buying tomato plants, I resist the ones that are already blooming. Those blossoms, as well as any little bitty tomatoes, will probably fall off anyway. Plants that are blooming or producing fruit have been in their pots too long. I want healthy roots, not blooms. I tap a plant out of the pot and look for healthy white roots, not a mushy rootbound tangle. I also look for stocky stems and leave tall spindly plants for less knowledgeable customers who should have done their homework.

Dig a hole for each plant, mixing into the soil an organic fertilizer or a balanced synthetic fertilizer and a large handful of dolomitic lime. Insufficient lime causes blossom-end rot, a discouraging and disgusting problem for tomato growers.

I have a neighbor who, year after year, overfertilizes his tomatoes with nitrogen and then wonders why he has lush, dark green plants and hardly any tomatoes. Heavy use of nitrogen promotes foliar growth and actually suppresses fruit formation. I have told him this in my usual tactful way, but he just cannot stop himself. Otherwise he is a perfect neighbor who grows delicious squash.

I place a tomato plant deep enough in the prepared hole so that only the top leaves are above ground, leaving plenty of stem beneath the soil line to develop roots. I continue to pinch off bottom leaves and sideshoots whenever I think of it.

Tomatoes Are for Everyone, Almost

I side-dress my tomato plants once or twice during the growing season with fish or seaweed emulsion and, after an initial deep soaking at planting time, provide at least an inch of water every week.

No room for tomatoes? Too much trouble to dig up a bed? Discouraged by nematodes? This is a trick I learned from garden writer, Jim Wilson. You will need a thirty-gallon plastic garbage can or wooden half-barrel. Two tomato plants grown in a container this size should provide a summer crop of ripe tomatoes plus end-of-season green tomatoes for pickles and frying.

Drill six half-inch drainage holes in the bottom of the container. Mix eight ounces of dolomitic limestone and fertilizer of your choice with thirty gallons of commercial potting mix (not potting soil or garden soil). Set the container on four bricks. Fill the container with potting mix to the top. Water thoroughly until you see water seeping from the drainage holes in the container's bottom. Place two tomato plants in the container.

Make a tomato cage of steel reinforcing wire eight feet tall and the same circumference as the container plus six inches for overlap. Wrap this cage around the container. Drive two steel fence posts into the ground and wire the cage to them. If an early frost threatens next fall, cover your cage with a blanket and, chances are, you could still be picking tomatoes at Thanksgiving. And won't that be something for which to be mighty thankful?

Tropical Pizzazz

Tropical is "in." Cottage garden is "out," until, of course, it is "in" again. We all know how that goes. Like ties, hemlines, and wines, gardens have trends, and why not? Fun-loving gardeners are always on the prowl for something new, so let the hunt for tropical pizzazz begin.

Tropical has the look of the rain forest. It is big and gaudy, with attitude. Intense colors vie shamelessly for attention: blood red, burgundy and purple, chartreuse and neon yellow. Oversized glossy leaves are splashed with patterns of splotches and stripes. Flashy and flamboyant and not a bit worried about tasteful. I love it.

Now, you and I are not likely to rip up our mixed borders and give our all to a tropical extravaganza. But we can perk up our borders with five or six hardy plants that will add tropical punch without turning our gardens into rain forests or color riots.

And we can start right now, in midsummer, to test whether this is a passing phase or real passion, in which case we may decide to rip out roses and phlox and go whole hog. In the meantime, we can add a few hardy plants to our gardens and see what they do for us.

Cannas come first. Nothing adds tropical pizzazz faster than these six- or seven-foot pillars of long strappy leaves and bold color. The good news is that they are hardy perennials that die back to the ground after hard frost but reappear in the spring in clumps. Begin with a single canna and next year you will have six, at least.

At one time, I disliked cannas. Their leaves were dull green and those flowers looked like globs of orange kleenex. They were okay as highway plantings, from a distance, but not in my backyard.

Cannas have come a long way and so have I. My first infatuation was *Canna* 'Bengal Tiger,' ripped from the ground by a sharing friend whose generosity comes to mind every time I look at the dozen or so now in my garden. *C.* 'Bengal Tiger' has green-and-gold striped leaves, edged with burgundy. The flowers are neon-orange and unabashedly gaudy. Some folks opt for discretion and remove them.

I have dug up quite a few of my own 'Bengal Tigers' for friends and I divide every year for a local plant sale, where last year I bought 'Australia,' a canna with burgundy-black leaves and blood-red blooms. Talk about exclamation points in the garden.

Cannas prefer sun or part sun and plenty of moisture, which is not to say they will fail to flourish if dry. Anything a state department of transportation plants in masses along the highways has got to be tough.

Like cannas, colocasias like sun or part sun, but they succeed in shade as well. Colocasias die back in winter and reappear in spring. They multiply with abandon, so you can have dramatic three- to four-foot clumps of colocasias and divide them occasionally to make more clumps.

Colocasias have another trait in common with cannas. They used to be plain green. We called them elephant ears. But now they wear charcoal leaves veined with green, variegated green leaves, silver edges, or creamy white splotches as well as stems that are red or black or variegated.

Alocasias look like colocasias with large heart-shaped leaves and thick stems but are generally not as hardy. Unless they are labeled as hardy in the zone where you garden, dig up the tubers and keep them in a protected place so they do not freeze over the winter.

You should be able to find both colocasias and cannas on sale in late summer at garden centers. Think of them as long-term investments and go for quality . . . and multiple stems that will put you on your way to a healthy clump.

If you are looking for a year-round tropical look, *Fatsia japonica* is for you. Fatsia has twelve-inch-wide glossy green leaves shaped like oversized maple leaves. This is not a flashy plant like cannas and colocasias, but they add tropical texture and broad sculptural mass to a shrub grouping or mixed border. The fall flowers are spiked creamy balls that remind me of little UFOs.

Another winter-hardy plant with a tropical look is *Aspidistra elatior.* Some people sneer at them, surely a hangover from the days when aspidistra was an overgrown, dusty houseplant in our grandmothers' parlors. For some reason, it is called cast iron plant.

Aspidistra is a fat clump of erect spiky leaves that grow about three to four feet tall. At least this is how it should be. If your aspidistra's leaves are tattered and stunted, give it plenty of compost, some fertilizer, and water. Cut the leaves down to the ground and let new foliage emerge. You will earn its gratitude, and aspidistra will gain your respect.

I have several clumps here and there, in shade and part shade, because I like aspidistra's sculptural upright posture. Mine are plain unexciting green . . . but I am pining for one of the new variegated forms. No one is going to sneer at them.

An often-neglected shrub you probably already have is the old-fashioned and overlooked evergreen aucuba with glossy dark green yellow-spattered foliage. For a touch of romance and added color, plant a male aucuba nearby and you will have shiny red berries added to the extravaganza.

Since 85 percent of the 10,000 fern species thrive in the tropics or subtropics, it is not surprising that ferns speak resonantly of the rain forest in a garden setting. Like ornamental grasses, they add complex texture and color shadings to the mix. Also like ornamental grasses, ferns have unpronounceable botanical names that life is too short for most of us to remember.

We see ferns most often in shaded areas, tucked among hostas, aspidistra, and shade-loving shrubs. Because most fern fronds are matte or unglossy, I like them combined with the shiny foliage of daphne and acanthus. Because they are so fine-textured, I like them next to broad-leafed shrubs such as fatsia, gardenias, and camellias.

Naturally I want ferns everywhere, and many of them will grow in the sun if the soil is rich in humus and adequate moisture is provided. Cinnamon fern, royal fern, sensitive fern, Southern shield fern, and hay-scented fern can go right into a sunny mixed border if they have to. So will silvery Japanese painted fern and a cultivar, 'Ursula's Red,' which has that same silvery coat, streaked with burgundy red. Talk about pizzazz.

Tender perennials, houseplants, and annuals such as plectranthus and coleus also add tropical allure. If you find bargains now, buy them and take cuttings before frost to over-winter if you have heated space to shelter them. Or build a greenhouse. What the heck.

However, cannas, colocasias, ferns, fatsia, aspidistra, and aucuba can be planted in the garden now for end-of-summer sprucing up, winter interest, and spring surprises. Hardy as they are, they have tropical attitude, and we know that in gardening, as in life, attitude is everything.

A Lust for Lantanas

Like that other old-fashioned shrub in our grandmothers' gardens, the hydrangea, lantanas have leapt into the horticultural market with a bang, gaining respectability among horticultural know-it-alls. Suddenly lantana varieties abound: upright, trailing, lavender, yellow, red, white, and rainbows of eye-popping hues.

Once snubbed as common and weedy, appropriate perhaps for white painted tires or old washtubs, lantana is making statements now in the fanciest and best-tended gardens owned by folks who know their plants.

And what a joy this plant is to know, as well as to grow. No matter how hot and dry the weather gets, lantana retains a sunny disposition, a role model for us all.

Lantana is native to tropical and subtropical regions and is considered a perennial in frost-free areas. In zone eight, where I garden, the upright varieties such as 'Miss Huff' and 'Athens Rose' are more likely to survive the winter than the trailing varieties. We do not consider any lantana a weed. Inelegant, maybe, but not a weed.

While most American gardeners have just recently been introduced to lantana varieties other than the standard multicolored shrub, as far back as 1700, more than fifty kinds had been named in the West Indies. Spanish colonists in the New World relied on lantanas for medicinal uses, making infusions to be taken internally or bathed in. I do not know what ailment was being treated, but I am not recommending the practice, since lantana is on current lists of poisonous plants.

The two lantana species we grow here are *L. camara,* which is upright (and hardier), and *L. montevidensis,* a trailing or weeping plant. *L. camara,* in tropical conditions, can grow twenty feet tall, but in our climate usually reaches just three or four feet. *L. montevidensis* is less than three feet tall and has weak stems that lie close to the ground, creating a spreading mass.

Camara or montevidensis, upright or trailing, these plants cover themselves with flowers from late spring to frost. From a distance, the blooms are flat circles of color but, if you look closely, you will see they are clusters of tiny trumpets, which explains their allure to butterflies.

Every year I plant a couple of trailing lantanas by our roadside mailbox, which is covered with another heat lover, orange trumpet vine. When not mowed down by the resident handyman, they have survived full sun, infrequent watering, and only a shawl of mulch for comfort.

Lantanas soak up the sun like Myrtle Beach lifeguards, but they also flourish in partial shade in my garden. They need well-drained soil, heat, very little fertilizer, and no water beyond that bestowed by Mother Nature. If you do fertilize with anything other than compost, use a slow-release low-nitrogen formula so you do not stimulate leaf growth and fewer flowers.

In addition to the lantanas out by the mailbox, I grow an assortment of trailing lantanas in the mixed borders and in containers. I like solid white and pale yellow, but the butterflies seem happy with any color. I also grow several upright lantanas in the border: 'Dallas Red,' 'Athens Rose,' and, of course, 'Miss Huff.'

'Miss Huff' blooms with gusto in the butterfly garden near the house. I like the story of 'Miss Huff' because it demonstrates that every garden has the potential to become a hotbed of new plant variations.

The real Miss Huff is Ruby Huff from Crawford, Georgia, which is in zone seven. Over thirty-five years ago, Ruby Huff planted generic lantanas on each side of her walkway. The two shrubs survived their first winter, so she pruned the dead-looking stems in spring after new growth appeared.

The lantanas flourished through the summer and survived a second winter. In spring, she cut them back. The bushes eventually grew six to seven feet tall and eight to ten feet wide each summer.

Miss Huff's lantanas came to the attention of Goodness Grows Nursery in Lexington, Georgia. After an especially bone-chilling winter with record low temperatures, the nurserymen decided that, if the plants survived, they would take cuttings and market the lantana as 'Miss Huff.' A star was born.

A Lust for Lantanas

'Miss Huff' now grows in millions of yards other than Miss Huff's to a height and width of just three to four feet, considerably smaller than Ruby's shrubs. The flowers open yellow, then switch to orange, and then fade to pink, so each cluster is a tricolored bouquet.

Note that Ruby Huff waited until spring to cut back her lantanas, and that is exactly what we should all do. When frost has turned the leaves brown, mulch but do not snip. Like those of the butterfly bush, lantana stems are hollow, so if water gets in and freezes, that may well be the end. Brace yourself and keep your hands off the pruners.

In spring, after the last frost, pull back the mulch and watch for new growth. When you see signs of life, and this may occur as late as mid-April, cut plants back to a foot or less.

Whether you get your lantanas through the winter or not, they are tough, handsome plants and well worth replanting every year if necessary. They look super in the garden and in containers, delighting the human population while attracting and sustaining butterflies as well—just another example of the satisfaction to be gained in a garden.

160

Mints Get a Bad Rap

I often have visitors walk around my garden with me and, as we stroll, I pull up a piece of this or that to give them. My guests seem appreciative and I enjoy being able to share. However, when I pull up a rooted sprig of a plant they have admired and tell them it is a mint, they frequently back away and say "No, thanks," as if I had offered them poison ivy.

Mints get an undeserved bad rap. They are attractive, delicious, and seductively scented, and they make fine groundcovers. While some spread enthusiastically, as a groundcover should, they pull up easily and can be discarded or shared.

Several years ago, a friend and I went to Callaway Gardens in Georgia and were disappointed that no plants were on sale so we could buy a souvenir of a pleasant weekend. On the way home, we stopped at a nursery and purchased chocolate mint (*Menta cv. x spicata*). I do not know what happened to hers, but mine has made itself at home far from its original site and every time I pull up a clump and get a whiff of York Peppermint Patty, I think of our trip together.

Chocolate mint is the most invasive of the mints but it is quite handsome with dark green foliage, chocolate brown stems, and an alluring calorie-free scent. Pulling it up is a sensual experience but, as a rule, I leave it unless it is crowding other plants.

Mints belong to the genus *Mentha*. Feel the stems and you will find four edges, as you do with salvias and sages, which are relatives. Most mints do not produce seed but spread by stolons.

Here is how it all began. Menthe was a nymph admired by the god Pluto. Proserpine, Pluto's wife, was understandably miffed, so she changed Menthe into the plant we now call mentha and banished her to the banks of a wandering stream. Too bad for Menthe, but good for the rest of us since mint has been a mainstay of our cuisine, our gardens, and our medicine chest, not to mention our chewing gum and juleps.

The Egyptian Pharisees paid taxes with mint. The Romans took mint to England, and mints have grown in English gardens ever since. Mint was strewn on the floors of castles, churches, and cottages as the first room deodorizers. In the Middle East, guests are still welcomed with cups of hot mint tea, and, in early American households, bundles of mint hung near the doorway to sweeten a guest's arrival.

Mints, like every herb I can think of, are happiest in well-drained soil. There is some argument over whether their oils are strongest when grown in sun or shade, but they will certainly grow in either.

I cut back mints mercilessly to encourage fresh growth. Mints that bloom, such as apple mint (*M. suaveolens*), should be cut back to prevent flowering since the aroma decreases when the plant concentrates on producing flowers. Just like us, there is a limit to how much mint can do at one time. You can actually use the mower or line trimmer to cut mint. No need to bother with clippers unless, like me, you enjoy getting down where the aroma is.

Many people grow mints in pots to keep them from spreading. Place the containers around the garden or group them for maximum effect, a different mint in each container. You can also cut the bottoms off pots and sink them into the soil so their stolons are discouraged (though not absolutely prevented) from wandering.

I never fertilize mints. I do not fertilize any herb once it is established. Mints thrive in moist soil (remember Menthe by the stream?) but seem to be okay in dry soil too. I have an apple mint that sneaks under the plastic covering of my greenhouse and spends summers, as well as winters, without a drop of water.

There are over 600 identified mint varieties and they all contain menthol. The smell and taste of each mint are determined by the proportion of menthol to other components. Mints are divided into two groups: peppermints, which are primarily menthol, and spearmints, which are primarily carovane, whatever that is.

Spearmints are not only better flavored, they are also better behaved as well and do not take over a garden when the gardener is away. The spearmint group (including pineapple and apple mints, my favorites) are used in tea, ice cream, jellies, and juleps. I love chopped apple mint in tabouli, a Mediterranean salad of cracked wheat, parsley, lemon, chives, and olive oil.

Peppermints are stronger in flavor, some overwhelmingly so, and are aggressive growers. Orange mint has broad, dark green leaves edged with purple and has a citrus scent and taste.

Another favorite of mine is Corsican mint (*M. requienii*), which is less than half an inch tall and forms a dense, emerald-green mat, a perfect filler between stepping stones. I also grow it in pots because I like the way Corsican mint rolls over the edges and mounds up in the middle like a pie.

Dwarf pennyroyal, another peppermint, is no taller than Corsican mint and makes the same kind of dense mat. I use it between stepping stones, at the edge of the border where it creeps out into the grass, and in pots under taller plants. I think you could make a lawn of dwarf pennyroyal since it spreads very quickly, can be mowed without damage, and, best of all, grows densely enough to choke out most weeds.

The next time someone offers you a handful of mint, take it home and plant it in an appropriate place, perhaps all around the foundation of your house to keep away snakes. Use a variety of mints in recipes, dry them for potpourri, and, best of all, enjoy them as attractive aromatic additions to your garden.

Just Give Me a Fig Tree and a Vine

Henry Mitchell, a writer I have admired since I discovered gardening, declared that the happiest human beings are those who own a fig tree and a vine.

Count us among the blessed. A twelve-foot-tall *Ficus carica* 'Celeste' lives in our yard, bringing delight to us, our neighbors, and the county's bird population. We rejoice in sharing our bounty since there is plenty for the taking, whether the takers are human or avian.

Every yard should have a fig tree of its own, not only for the fruit but also because of its lush foliage and strong, sculptural form. Our golf-ball-sized figs are delicious. I occasionally make fig preserves and even fig cake. We like them best, however, right from the tree. So does Katie, our Labrador retriever, who scouts daily during fig season for figs that have reached the peak of ripeness.

A fig tree is absolutely care-free and without pests, except for an occasional squirrel who is as welcome as the birds to nibble. Our tree thrives though it has never been fertilized, sprayed, or pampered in any way.

Recently on television I watched in horror as a poor gardener in Ontario prepared his dozen fig trees for the winter. He bent each tree over until it fit into a ditch, which he then covered with soil and sheets of attic insulation. I am not making this up. First he had to clip and tie the trees, uproot them, and stomp on them so they fit into the ditch. Why in the world would a person who loves figs this much live in Ontario instead of a more temperate climate?

It is worth watching television occasionally to make us appreciate life. Like most Southerners, I gripe about the heat in July and August and drought-like conditions that seem worse every year. However, I know we are blessed with a growing season of nine or ten months and something in bloom all year.

My guess is that the fellow in Ontario may curse the cold but counts his blessings every time he eats a fig and finds joy in every fig tree that makes it through winter. Gardeners everywhere are a grateful lot.

When Henry Mitchell wrote about the happiness a vine can bring, he was talking specifically about a grapevine. We have seven or eight grapevines, but those are my husband's bailiwick. My vines are delightfully decorative though inedible as far as I know. But they certainly keep me smiling.

On my mailbox is *Campsis xtagliabuana* 'Mme. Galen,' which, in good conscience, I cannot recommend for a structure less than thirty feet. This vine grows with gusto. It is unstoppable. I control mine with clippers, but at times during the summer cars swerve in front of my house to avoid outreaching stems. The flowers are bright orange and attractive to ants, bees, and hummingbirds, though perhaps not to mailmen. Our mailman calls it "cow itch." The seedpods are long bean-like things that I remove. If they ever got away from me, I fear the county would be covered by Mme. Galen's offspring.

Two other perennial vines that threaten to take over my yard if my attention wanders are sweet autumn clematis and passionflower vine. Their babies pop up everywhere but are easily extracted. The trick is to walk your garden frequently, but why would you garden if you do not take the time to do this? As you stroll, just pull up strays.

I recommend this method for all weeds and vegetative runaways. Lean over, grasp the intruder, and give an appropriate tug. This strategy is cheap, is environmentally safe, and increases flexibility, qualities that cannot be claimed by Round Up and its ilk.

Another couple of perennial vines I favor are five-leafed akebia, which has small dark pink blooms in March and April, and hops vine, which I hope will someday have hops. So far, all I have enjoyed is glorious chartreuse foliage, which reminds me of England. Perhaps I should not ask for more.

Of course I grow confederate jasmine. It climbs our front porch and an arbor leading to the mixed border. I visited a friend's garden recently and she was growing confederate jasmine up a pine tree. Why did I not think of doing this years ago? Can you imagine the scent when the jasmine is in bloom and a gentle breeze blows?

Last summer I fell in love with gloriosa lily (*Gloriosa rothschildiana*) when I saw it twining through shrubs at a botanical garden. This spectacular vine has complex lily-like red flowers edged in gold. I have three planted in my own garden this year and cannot wait to see them start their voyage upward. I hope they reproduce lustily so I can have hundreds all over my neighborhood.

If I had a fence around my yard, it would be covered with vines but, as it is, I have to search out upright structures for vine growing. The sweet autumn clematis grows on an unused clothesline along with a Lady Banksia rose at the opposite end. Passionflower climbs a telephone pole and whatever else it chooses. Akebia and hops grow on seven-foot wooden T's my husband built.

Annual vines I grow are *Asarina* 'Joan Lorraine' with blue tubular blooms that begin in midsummer and continue until a hard freeze, and cypress vine with red blooms adored by hummingbirds, butterflies, and me. Asarina grows about six feet while cypress vine reaches twenty feet if encouraged. Both are reseeders.

I do not limit myself to floral vines. I purchased two bean towers for snow peas and beans and perhaps a few gourds. I am considering planting gourds and hyacinth beans on my neighbor's fence between our yards. A gardener does what a gardener has to do.

That empty upright space beckons. I only wish their fence were taller.

Henry Mitchell was right, as usual. I am, indeed, a happy woman who possesses not only more grapevines than I want, but also a fig tree and a dozen ornamental vines to adorn my garden and enrich my soul.

166

Put It in a Pot

August is a tough month for gardeners. The heat has gotten to us and to our plants, so full of hope when we put them in the earth last spring. Now they look disheveled, perhaps even moribund, and there seems little point in replacing them or starting over.

It may seem too late to start a new summer border or even reclaim an old one, but this is an ideal time to start container gardens to see us through fall and even winter if we select the right plants. What I like best about container gardens is that you can have a lot of fun designing and redesigning with minimal effort and expense.

Step one in creating an interesting container garden is to choose a large pot. The larger the pot, the less frequently you have to water and the more varied the plants can be.

Be sure the container you choose has several holes in the bottom. Drainage is crucial. You can put a layer of rocks, gravel, or crushed shells in the bottom for extra drainage but, if the pot bottom has holes and you have used appropriate soil, it is not necessary.

For soil, my preference is not soil at all but two-thirds peat-based potting mix and one-third mushroom compost or your own humusy garden soil. Add a handful or two of dried manure, organic fertilizer, or slow-release fertilizer pellets.

Since container gardening became trendy, the common wisdom has been that soil mix must be dumped every year and containers should be refilled with fresh soil mix and nutrients. I suspect most gardeners never followed this advice and neither did I, since dumping and replacing strike me as wasteful, expensive, and laborious.

We certainly do not replace the soil in our gardens unless it has been contaminated. We amend soil with nutrients and we improve moisture retention by adding compost. That is exactly what we should do with the soil mix in containers: Treat it like dirt.

I mulch my container gardens with finely shredded pinebark or an inch or two of pebbles. When I add new plants, which is half the ongoing fun of container gardening, I dig in additional compost and amendments or slow-release fertilizer. Otherwise, I water when the top two inches of the soil are dry and watch the garden thrive.

The challenge begins with the selection of plants. The basic formula is simple but effective: something tall, something round, and something trailing. I have a creative friend who adds a fourth dimension: something chartreuse. She has a point. Like it or not, chartreuse perks a garden up. So does yellow.

This same friend walks around garden centers with her cart full of plants, physically combining as she shops. I imagine her muttering the mantra: "Tall, round, trailing, chartreuse." Not only does she check the outdoor plants; she hits the house plant aisles as well.

A favorite container garden of mine is one I have used on my front porch for years. The combination is aspidistra (cast iron plant), holly fern, and variegated jasmine, all of which are evergreen. It is not breathtaking but it is dependable, completely winter-hardy, and an interesting mix of forms and textures. In spring daffodils pop through, and in summer annuals add color.

Another combination I like is dracena (from the house plant department), chartreuse globe arborvitae, variegated chameleon plant, and white-flowered bacopa. Unlike the aspidistra and holly fern combination, this has to be taken apart before frost since dracena is not winter-hardy. But that is okay. We gardeners know nothing in life is permanent.

I can replace the dracena in the container with laurel, myrtle, serissa, a small pine, rosemary, or anything else that is upright and will give my container height and oomph. Instead of bacopa I could use lamium, thyme, or another low-growing trailer. Instead of the arborvitae, which I plan to move into the mixed border, I could use mums, giant red mustard, or Swiss chard.

Whatever you plant, plant them closer together than you would in the border and use larger plants to make an immediate impact. You can, of course, use small plants and watch them grow, but instant gratification has its rewards and, in the case of container gardens, is neither fattening nor immoral.

A trick I learned from a photographer is to move large containers into bare spots, placing them on upended pots or blocks to give them height. Now I keep handy a couple of well-packed containers for this purpose. You never know when a hole in the border might appear . . . but it is usually when company is coming.

I often dig up plants from my garden for late-season containers. However, in August, garden centers are anxious to decrease summer inventories, so I also shop around and treat myself to daring combinations and good buys.

I have learned most of what I know about garden design from puttering around with container gardens. By selecting and switching around plants of varied textures, colors, growth patterns, and shapes, a gardener develops a feel for what is pleasing and interesting. Before she knows it, she is applying the same creative principles in her borders with surprising and satisfying results.

Just think in terms of tall, round, and trailing. Look for interesting zingy combinations of textures and colors, in foliage as well as flowers. By all means, have fun, think creatively, and live for the moment, at least until winter sets in.

Put It in a Pot

More, Gotta Have More

Here I go, confessing again. I am guilty of greed. But so is every other genuinely obsessed gardener I know.

We have this compulsion to own more plants than our ground will hold or our budgets will tolerate. We agonize over seed catalogs, good sense telling us that we really should not order odontonema or musa ensete, but our insatiable appetite wins out and we wind up with more seeds than we can possibly plant and exotic choices suitable only for glass conservatories staffed by full-time gardeners.

We wander through nurseries, our eyes sparkling as we sniff and fondle the merchandise, imagining each plant gracing our own borders. There is always room in our gardens. If not, another plot of ground is ready for expansion.

Unlike greed for money or food, gardening greed is beneficial to the environment and to other gardeners. While gardeners want it all, we differ from misers and gourmands because, once we have a plant, we like to share.

We root our favorites, divide our treasures, save seeds of prize specimens, and, as soon as someone admires our success, we insist on divvying up our booty. I have never known a selfish gardener nor one who refuses to reveal the secrets of his success to anyone who shows a glimmer of interest.

In fact, we can be pretty darn boring about the tricks of our hobby. Admire our vines or hostas and you are apt to find out a good deal more about plant choices, fertilization, and slug damage than anyone in his right mind wants to know.

Many of my favorite plants are the offspring of friends' gardens. Not only do the plants look nifty in my borders, but they are also reminders of people and places I love. One favorite place is the Elizabethan Gardens in Manteo, North Carolina. On my first visit there when I was just beginning to garden, one of the workers was pruning lacecap hydrangeas, which I had never seen before.

Since I was new to begging, I shyly asked if I might have a cutting. The gardener handed me a dozen, pleased by my admiration of the garden and my curiosity about his work. Though we never exchanged names, he became a lifelong friend because I am grateful to him every time I look at the results of those cuttings.

I wrapped those hydrangea cuttings in wet paper towels and stuck them in a plastic cup. I have since learned to carry an ample plastic bag (as well as a pocketknife) everywhere I go. Before leaving home, I put water in the plastic bag, shake it, then dump the water out and seal the bag. The remaining droplets are all the moisture needed to keep cuttings fresh.

I have a friend with an otherwise impeccable reputation for honesty who carries plastic bags on his world travels, snipping cuttings and gathering seedheads in some of the world's most renowned gardens, and then smuggling them home to his own borders. This is real gardener's greed. This fellow risks all to own a plant he covets, but then shares his winnings happily with those of us too honorable or cowardly to risk our passports.

I myself have taken a seedhead or two if there are lots of them on the plant. If seedlings are coming up in a walkway, I figure they are fair game. I have discovered that theft is unnecessary, however. I have never been turned down when I asked for a cutting from a plant I admired in a friend's garden or even a public garden.

I have kept cuttings in plastic bags for a week before doing anything else with them. I keep them cool in an ice chest, refrigerator, or air-conditioned hotel room and, when I am ready to root them, the cuttings seem ready too. I have already trimmed off all but the top four or six leaves of a cutting before I bagged it. I also cut the remaining leaves in half (horizontally) to reduce transpiration or stress since the stems are rootless.

Fill a bottomless rooting box (made from four boards nailed together), a plastic pot, or a planter with coarse sand, vermiculite, perlite, finely shredded pine bark, or a combination of any of these. This is the "medium" where cuttings become growing plants through the miracle of propagation.

Whichever container you use, it needs to have excellent drainage and be kept in a shaded location. The medium should remain consistently moist but not soggy. Since the climate is humid where I garden,

I do not cover my cuttings with plastic, but I check them almost every day to make sure the medium does not dry out. If I were propagating in the desert, I would use plastic covering.

When I am ready to start the rooting process, I recut the stem just below a growing node, wet the end, and dip it into rooting hormone, which you can buy anywhere that sells gardening supplies. I stick each cutting into the medium whose sole purpose is to hold the stem upright and give the roots someplace to wander once they emerge.

After three or four weeks, I tug gently on each cutting. If it resists the tug, the cutting has roots. If not, I leave it alone and tug again in a couple of weeks. After the cutting is rooted, I transplant it into a pot filled with two-thirds potting mix and one-third compost.

If the cutting fails to root in a couple of months or if it begins to look puny, toss it out of the rooting container but definitely try again. What have you got to lose?

I usually wait two or three seasons before I put a newly rooted shrub out on its own and, if you have dogs or children, I suggest you do the same. Annuals rooted in early summer can go in the garden by late summer. Perennials rooted in summer can be moved to the garden in fall or the following spring, or you can keep them in pots until the mood strikes or the moon is right.

June through September are the optimum months for taking cuttings but, addicted as I am, I begin in March and continue until November. All a propagator needs is a sharp eye, a few plastic bags, a pocketknife, and a friendly manner. A wistful look is also helpful.

For an investment of less than $10 for medium, hormone, and a container, you will be ready to create your own Eden and a priceless collection of botanical memories.

A Wandering Mind Wants to Grow

Gardeners always have something to do, and no sooner do we start a project than we start planning the next one. We begin one task and are inevitably drawn to another.

Just this morning I walked out to my garden to deadhead stokesia. If you want perennials and annuals to keep perking, you have to clip the spent blossoms. Otherwise, they start setting seed and think they are through for the summer. Keep deadheading and most of them will bloom again . . . and again.

I stopped to clip a few cuttings from the Mexican orange shrub (*Choysia ternata*). I like to have rooted cuttings or plants to give to visitors who admire its year-round golden foliage and white flowers that look like little orange blossoms. I remind myself to make a note on my garden calendar to cut this shrub almost to the ground next winter to stimulate branching. It looks a little skimpy. I put the cuttings in a plastic bag.

But I digress, as I do whenever I head out to the garden with a particular task in mind. As I settled down to tidy up the stokesia, I discovered ferny little *Coreopsis* 'Moonbeam' seedlings popping up here and there, so, of course, I had to locate a container, maneuver the seedlings out of the soil, and take them to the picnic table where I do my potting.

After potting up the coreopsis, I put them in a shady spot so they could rest before I move them to a sunny location. I then checked my rooting box and, sure enough, several hydrangea cuttings were putting out new growth. Time to pot them up, too.

Since I did not have rooting hormone with me, I stuck the choysia cuttings in the medium, intending to come back later to do a proper propagating job.

Finally I returned to my deadheading, but only after stopping to pull up a few weeds, add mulch to the front of the border, and check on some Swallowtail caterpillars devouring parsley. I put a few of them, along with some lush green parsley stems, into a plastic container to give to the little boy next door.

Every child or child-at-heart should have the joy of raising and releasing butterflies. Give the caterpillars a protective container covered with screen or netting and watch them munch parsley or fennel or other appropriate fodder (placed in a small jar of water to keep it fresh). Watch the caterpillars form chrysalises suspended from a branch that you have also placed in the container.

In a couple of weeks, the butterflies emerge. To share this metamorphosis and to release a butterfly from your finger near a clump of flowers is one of life's richest experiences.

I returned to the deadheading only to realize that the *Artemisia lactiflora* had overgrown its spot and needed to be dug, divided, and moved. These divisions also needed replanting or potting up. I know it is midsummer and not time to divide perennials, but sometimes desperate measures must be taken and the artemisia needed to be moved today.

The corner of the border that gets full sun much of the day needed watering. And then the tomatoes had to be picked. While I did that, I decided to clip some suckers to root for a late crop. I do this every year with little success, but it seems such a promising and frugal idea that I continue to try.

The stokesia is finally deadheaded and I have done a dozen other things in the process. And that is exactly what happens as I write: I begin talking about herbs and wind up thinking about the maple tree; I start a serious discussion of soil improvement and my thoughts drift to roses; I get going on deadheading stokesia and wind up with tomatoes.

Here it is, the middle of summer, and here am I, thinking of Christmas. For years I have decorated our Christmas tree with creamy white baby's breath, saving stems from flower arrangements and even buying a bouquet of it just for tree trimming. But last year I used sea lavender statice (*Limonium latifolum*) from my own garden and liked it even more.

Naturally, one adornment led to another. I started to put dried hydrangeas on our tree, stuffing the blooms into skimpy spots. Although it is tempting, I do not spray them gold or anything fancy. I prefer the mottled purple and pale green shades they turn without my interference.

You probably see where I am going with this. Once again in my life, one thing is leading to another, and next year (or maybe the year after) I am going to have nothing but ornaments from my garden on our tree, except of course the lights. There is a limit to my yen for simplicity.

Toward this festive end, I am growing lots of clover-like gomphrena and red and gold *Celosia cristata* that looks like brains made out of velvet. I will add the colors and textures of yarrow, grasses, love-lies-bleeding, teasel, larkspur, and statice. Rosemary, thyme, sweet annie (*Artemisia annua*), and lavender will emit subtle herbal scents. Translucent seedpods of money plant (*Lunaria annua*) will give our tree a silvery glow.

The possibilities are limitless and exciting. Just think of all the pods and cones and foliage that can dress a tree. I do not even have to grow my Christmas decorations. I can simply scour the fields and woods and the gardens of people who think nothing gorgeous happens in a garden once frost hits.

But what to do with all those ornaments we have amassed: souvenirs from travel, our children's crafts, gifts from good friends? For the past few years, I have invited our grandchildren to each take an ornament from our tree to add to their personal collections. Passalong ornaments, I guess you would call them.

So soon our tree will not be adorned with shiny glass and small toys and glitter. It will be filled instead by the bounty of our earth and the gifts of nature. And soon my mind will meander in a different direction, to new tasks and new opportunities. A gardener's plate, thank heaven, is never empty.

Herbs with Allure

Some think the scent of summer is roses. Some think gardenias. For me, nothing smells of summer more than basil. If basil were inedible and ugly, I would still grow it for the incomparable pleasure of sticking my nose into a basil bouquet and breathing deeply. This is one intoxicating plant.

Fortunately, basil not only smells wonderful, it is also a gorgeous plant with satiny emerald green leaves that renew themselves as you snip them for pesto, tomato sandwiches, and other basil-flavored delights. Genovese basil is my favorite, for cooking as well as for its kelly green glossy foliage in the mixed border.

Of course, there are dozens of basils . . . spicy Thai basil, lettuce leaf basil, globe-shaped basil, lemon basil, and African blue. You could have an entire garden of basil plants, which is not a bad idea.

The Thai basil 'Siam Queen' is a cultivar I grow for butterflies as much as for myself. This herb, with its upright maroon blooms and sturdy stems, definitely belongs in the flower border as well as in arrangements. The leaves are about an inch long and do not look like basil leaves, but one sniff tells you it is definitely basil, with a hint of pepper.

Basil does have its downsides. As a tender annual, its season is much too short to suit me, unless you winter it over in a greenhouse much warmer than mine or on a sunny windowsill. Unlike oregano and other herbs, basil does not retain its flavor when dried. The best way to preserve it is to make a pesto of olive oil and basil and freeze cubes or small containers of it so that you will have sufficient basil flavor and aroma to tide you over until next spring.

I am not a happy cook (although I am an enthusiastic eater). I scramble around and usually get food on the table at appropriate times, but, if I had a choice, I would never cook. I mean NEVER. Other than basil and perhaps thyme, my interest in herbs is far from culinary.

I do, however, admire the usefulness of herbs. No one ever asks me how I use a petunia or an acanthus, but, whenever I talk about herbs, the question inevitably comes: "What do you do with it?"

Herbs by definition are useful, not only for cooking but also for medicating, dyeing, repelling insects, covering up unpleasant odors, and warding off evil. Herbs are decorative and aromatic in wreaths and bridal bouquets as well as in flower arrangements. Certain herbs, such as tansy, repel insects, but even better are the herbs, such as fennel and garlic chives, that attract beneficial insects who spend their days devouring evil doers and pollinating food crops.

As for me, I grow herbs primarily for the pleasure of their company. I love their fragrances and the textures they add. I enjoy their diverse uses and attractiveness to butterflies, hummingbirds, and bees who make a garden cheerful and dynamic.

Years ago I discovered sweet annie (*Artemisia annua*), a reseeding annual that smells wonderful. It starts out as a miniscule seedling and grows to six feet by midsummer. The foliage is ferny and the shape is that of a soft, loose Christmas tree. At the end of summer, it forms "flowers" that look like tiny beads. Let the plant dry in the garden (to a rich bronze color), and you will have seedlings galore the following spring.

But do not leave it all in the garden. Cut sweet annie to bring into the house and let its fragrance permeate the air. Make dried arrangements and wreaths of it. I have a sweet annie wreath that must be ten years old. It is a bit dusty but still has remnants of the sweet, spicy scent it had in the garden.

Another reseeding annual herb I like is borage with sky-blue flowers that attract bees. You wonder why I want to attract bees? Ask any farmer who has to purchase or rent bees to pollinate his crops because of the diminishing bee population.

Borage flowers are edible, tasting a bit like cucumber, and are a pretty addition to salads, punch, and iced tea. The mature plant is about thirty inches tall and wide. I put mine near my tomatoes, hoping those bees will be as busy as they are supposed to be. Buy a plant this year and let it reseed, or save seeds to start several borage plants next spring.

My favorite perennial herb is lavender although, like most gardeners in hot and humid climates, I have trouble keeping it alive and attractive. A few years ago, I read a column by Madalene Hill, coauthor of *Southern Herb Growing*, who also has had trouble growing lavender satisfactorily. It is almost always comforting to know we are not alone in our difficulties.

Most herbs have three basic needs: sun, slightly alkaline soil, and good drainage. While I have found other herbs to be flexible and forgiving, lavender is uncompromising about all three conditions. Lavender wants moisture around its roots but dry foliage. This is why most lavenders become leggy by midsummer. Their bottoms stay wet and leaves fall off in despair.

Lavender needs mulch (remember it wants moist roots) that dries quickly and reflects heat to keep those bottom leaves dry. Madalene Hill tried coarse builder's sand, white granite chips, and pea gravel and all three worked, but pea gravel looked best. She now spreads a two- to three-inch layer of gravel around each lavender plant. Hill did not say so, but the pea gravel may also maintain the soil alkalinity lavender prefers.

I just looked again at Madalene Hill's article, which I had saved. I am pleased to see how sprightly she looks in her photograph since, like me, she is getting up in years. This reinforces my premise that gardeners stay young longer in mind, heart, and body because we are always planning ahead. The evidence is there on Hill's joyful face and in the fact that she is still out there in Texas hill country, solving problems and planning next year's garden.

Save Me a Salvia

If plant families had reunions, the genus *Salvia*, with over 900 species growing all over the world, would be a mob scene. I do not know who counts species, but I know how to tell what is or is not a salvia. Like mint, which is close enough kin to be a reunion guest, salvias have square stems.

The words salvia and sage seem interchangeable with both names evolving from the Latin word *salvere*, which means "to be saved" as in salvation. "Sage" comes to us via Old English and is associated with wisdom. It would be comforting to know that salvia makes us wise and keeps us safe, but I cannot promise that. I do know, however, that it keeps bees, butterflies, and hummingbirds deliriously happy.

I grow more salvia varieties in my garden than any other genus and I might be content with a border of nothing but salvias. I would not be thrilled, but I would not be miserable.

My first salvia was *S. farinacea* 'Victoria,' a velvety blue bloomer I started from seeds. If you cannot say farinacea, call it mealycup sage. This common name comes from the miniscule white hairs that make the flower look mealy or floury. This is what I call an "ephemeral perennial," returning for several years in my garden but then, for no apparent reason, giving up the ghost. 'Victoria' grows to about twenty-four to thirty inches in height and width, loves the sun, and is just about drought-proof.

The next salvia I planted was *S. uliginosa* or bog sage, referring, I suppose, to its odd marshy odor. This is a spreader, but wandering stems pull up easily. In fact, it is when you are pulling them up that you realize how bad bog sage smells. But its odor is compensated for by attractive blue and white blooms on four- to five-foot stems. I do not recall where my first plant came from, but I know *S. ulignosa* has been in my garden in several locations over fifteen years. I regard bog sage as a "perennial perennial."

Without question, my favorite salvia is *S. guaranitica*, which has royal blue blooms, some of them at eye level making it handy for hummingbird watching. The nectar must be divine because I have stood less than a foot away from a hummingbird so intent upon guzzling that it ignores my presence. This kind of experience reminds a gardener why she gardens.

S. guaranitica (anise sage) is hard to beat for color, but then I am partial to royal blue. Two cultivars are light blue 'Argentina Skies' and dark purple 'Black and Blue,' but these colors exist in other flowers. Royal blue is scarce as hen's teeth and, boy, does it add punch in the border.

Like bog sage, *S. guaranitica* is wont to wander but pulls up easily, which is good because everyone who sees it wants some. When you are pulling plants up to share or to pot up, look for small plants. If no small plants are to be found, pull up a medium-sized one and cut it back to the first robust foliage on the stem. When foliage eventually appears at soil level, cut off the long stem. This trim will produce a fuller, multistemmed plant.

In August, another favorite salvia appears in my borders: *S. coccinea* 'Lady in Red,' which I have not planted for years because she appears like magic from self-sown seeds. 'Lady in Red' is not to be confused with that annual stiff-necked red salvia lined up like soldiers in a flower border. That is *S. splendens*, and I choose not to discuss it.

S. leucantha or Mexican bush sage blooms in my garden from mid-August until frost, grows about four feet tall and wide, and has long spikes of purple or purple mixed with white. This is a flower that calls out "cut me, cut me" for arrangements. To over-winter Mexican bush sage, after it finally gives up in late fall, do not cut the stems off but cover the crown with at least eight inches of mulch. It may return the following spring.

Another late-blooming salvia and hummingbird favorite is pineapple sage (*S. elegans*). Unfortunately, it blooms around Labor Day, so hummingbirds do not have long to enjoy it in my garden. However, I am happy it blooms when it does, providing something new to admire in the garden. The leaves, when crushed, do indeed smell like pineapple although they taste like grass.

Garden designers look down their noses, I notice, at the old *S. superba*, perhaps because it is tough enough to be hardy north of zone seven and neither heat nor drought bothers it. I have an *S. superba* I am unable to identify. It has large fuzzy basal leaves and bright blue blooms that appear sporadically in March and continue to appear until the first freeze. I appreciate its tenacity, but then I am not a snob. Horticulturally or otherwise.

Salvias appreciate a little afternoon shade and moisture, but obligingly survive in the hot sun with an occasional soaking. As I do with all annuals and perennials, I whack off a quarter to a third of each plant with hedge shears when I tire of deadheading individual spent blooms. They recover quickly and put forth more effort.

Multistemmed salvias (like *S. superba*) are easily divided. The others are a cinch to propagate from stem cuttings. Before frost, take six-inch tip cuttings from stems that are not flowering. You can carry them through the winter as cuttings or, once they have rooted, pot up the cuttings in potting mix. Either way, put them in a sunny location where you can keep them from freezing.

Whether your salvias are annual, perennial, or ephemeral, they require little effort and expenditure in exchange for color, texture, and hummer sustenance. That is what I call a sage bargain.

Save Me a Salvia

Secret to Success: Succulents

Remember the scene in the movie *The Graduate* when his father's friend shares with young Benjamin the ultimate secret of success? He leans toward the new Harvard grad and says, man-to-man and somewhat drunkenly, the single magic word: "Plastics."

Well, here am I, ready to share, gardener-to-gardener and cold-sober, my own secret to guaranteed success: succulents. You just cannot go wrong with these bulletproof beauties. Tough as they are, succulents are extraordinarily attractive plants, available in a variety of colors, shapes, and sizes, and, because of coast-to-coast drought conditions in recent years, they are definitely cutting edge.

When I say "succulents" I am not talking about cactus, which I regard as unwieldy and more threatening than plants should be. I am referring to sedums, sempervivums, and agaves. They all have thick juicy leaves and stems, which is why they are called succulent. In these leaves and stems, they store moisture so they are capable of surviving long periods of drought that defeat more fragile flora.

Not only do I combine sempervivums, sedums, and agaves in pots, but I also lump them in my mind as succulents because, frankly, I have trouble remembering which is which. This is not a big problem since they all have the same growing requirements. They are happy no matter how dry or hot it is but, then again, they are also content and especially attractive when covered with frost. They thrive in full sun but seem comfortable in shade.

One problem they will not tolerate, however, is poor drainage, especially in the winter. Grow succulents in a mixture of sand and potting mix and, if you have them in pots, make sure the bottoms have sufficient drainage holes. I let the soil dry out completely and then I saturate them. While they survive well without pampering, they respond gratefully to a little attention and judicious fertilizing.

You can plant succulents directly in the ground as well as in pots and they will flourish. Dwarf sedums, such as variegated or golden *sedum acre*, take to open ground with enthusiasm, spreading into mats that make interesting groundcovers. They have almost negligible root systems, so they are easy to pull up if they should happen to wander beyond bounds.

In my garden I grow a group of succulents in a corner by the garage, the hottest place in the yard. The only water they get is rain, and we all know how rare that often is. They are in full sun all day and they have never been pampered, let alone fertilized.

My favorite way to grow succulents is in large, flat, bowl-shaped containers that I place here and there in places that are rarely watered. The wider the container the better. For drainage and style, nothing beats terra cotta, though I also use plastic and hypertufa planters as well as a wooden salad bowl with holes drilled in the bottom.

The artist in my soul emerges as I mix round plump sempervivums with tiny sedums and pointy-leafed agaves. The combinations of shapes and colors are immensely satisfying and easy to accomplish. I relish such rare instant gratification and guaranteed success.

Sempervivums are commonly called hens-and-chicks since they resemble a setting hen with a brood of biddies under her. The mother plant is a tight rose that surrounds itself with tiny rosettes. Propagation could not be easier. Just ease out rosettes, poke a bit of stem into sandy soil, and you soon have a new setting hen.

A second name for sempervivums is "houseleeks" since in England and Ireland they were planted on rooftops to ward off fires. They are still used as medicinal herbs to relieve burns.

Unlike sempervivums, sedum leaves are rounded rather than spiny. Sedums, perhaps because of their ability to grow in inhospitable soil, are also called stonecrops. They are used increasingly in perennial borders and landscape plantings. *Sedum* 'Autumn Joy' and *S.* 'Neon' are about fifteen inches tall and have large pale pink flower heads that become deep rose by the end of summer. *S.* 'Purple Emperor' has leaves tinged with purple. Other sedums have variegated leaves and still others, such as golden *S. mackinoi* 'Ogon,' are less than an inch tall with leaves just a quarter inch long.

Agaves or century plants are my favorites because they are dramatically sculptural. A ghost-gray agave makes a statement. Sometimes a big one. *Agave salmiana* matures to five feet in height and the flower spikes, which look like asparagus on steroids, reach twenty-five feet. Like sempervivums, agaves produce small duplicates of themselves, ripe for expansion. The adaptability of evergreen succulents is not surprising since most sedums and sempervivums come from European and Asian mountain ranges and agaves come from the mountainous regions of the American Southwest.

Whether succulents are planted in the ground or in containers, I mulch them with pea gravel or small pebbles to keep their bottom leaves off the soil. Too much moisture, especially in cold temperatures, leads to rot and ultimate demise.

Of course, now that I have become enthralled with succulents, I want lots of them and keep discovering new specimens at nurseries, botanical gardens, and even big discount chains where they are often hidden among houseplants.

Fortunately, succulents are not expensive and, since they are so easy to propagate, you get a lot of bang for the buck if you are resourceful. If you are really resourceful, you can pinch a bit from other gardeners' succulent collections to begin your own.

Then sit back and watch the show. Let the wind blow and the sun bake. No insects, diseases, or fungi to fight. I would not want a whole garden of succulents but it sure is pleasant to have something green (and gray and gold and bronze) to count on, no matter what summer or winter brings.

❧

184

Crepe or Crape? I'll Take Both

I hesitate to bring up the subject of trees during the summer since I myself avoid planting trees, shrubs, and perennials while the heat is on.

However, this is definitely the time to talk about crepe myrtles since they are such stars of the summer landscape. And what long-blooming, brilliant stars they are. No wonder we are swept up in the urge to have one or two or a dozen, though we know we should wait until fall to give them the right conditions in our gardens.

My recommendation is that you select crepe myrtles while they are in bloom and keep them comfortable in dappled shade, still in their well-watered containers, until fall. If the crepe myrtle is root-bound, repot it in a larger container. Roots escaping from the bottom of the pot are worthless, so cut them off. If the pot is a tangle of roots and the soil is skimpy, massage the roots or take a knife and cut through them. Cutting the roots stimulates generation of new feeder roots, and that is exactly the kind you want.

About the spelling of "crepe," I have seen genuine certified experts spell it either way. I opt for c-r-e-p-e because the petals resemble crepe paper or silk crepe fabric, but wiser minds than mine think they are crape myrtles. Michael Dirr, generally regarded as The Authority on woodies, calls them crape myrtles in his *Manual of Woody Landscape Plants*. Of course, we could call them *Lagerstroemia indica* or *L. fauriei* and cut off the argument.

You can imagine my dismay when I drove into my own son's imaginatively landscaped yard and saw that he, like other well-intentioned but misguided gardeners, had chopped off the limbs of his crepe myrtles. I knew this kind of thing happened in other people's families, but I never expected to see such mutilation in a Rochester yard.

But there they were, pricey trees with gorgeous exfoliating cinnamon bark and silky gray trunks, their formerly graceful branches now stumps. Stumps! The shapes are forever mangled since from these stumps will come bunches of puny vertical branches.

When I see crepe myrtles butchered this way, I cannot help thinking of arms cut off midway between wrist and elbow and fingers growing out from the stumps. Not a pretty picture, especially considering how absolutely perfect a naturally shaped crepe myrtle is.

Now here is the real crime. My son was actually advised by his local nursery to do this amputation, and I am at a loss to know why. Crepe myrtles are the only flowering trees we treat this way. We would not think of chopping off the branches of a dogwood or flowering cherry.

Supposedly, crepe myrtles bloom more prolifically when their branches are amputated each spring. I doubt it, especially when I see abundantly floriferous unclipped specimens. But even if they should bloom better for a few summer months, when they lose their leaves in the fall they are atrocities instead of gracefully spreading forms that enhance the winter landscape.

I do not believe it myself, but more cynical folks suggest that landscapers recommend this mutilation because they are short on jobs to do for clients in late winter. I think the custom started at shopping centers (major clients for landscapers) and spread to strip malls, gas stations, fast food restaurants, and, alas, eventually to suburban yards.

Some crepe myrtle mutilation occurs to keep the plant properly sized for its location. When shopping for crepe myrtles, look carefully at the tags that should tell you the mature height of the plant and its growth habit. If you choose the correct crepe myrtle, you should never (or rarely) have to prune it.

You can select crepe myrtles that will be foot-high groundcovers or three-foot shrubs all their lives, or crepe myrtles that will become ten-foot trees in a few years. Or you can plant crepe myrtles that will eventually become thirty-five-foot trees. This is as broad a range in a single plant group that I know of, so you have the opportunity to select one tailor-made for your landscape.

Furthermore, you can select the shape: globose, spreading, arching, upright, or pendulous. This most obliging ornamental blooms in shades from pale pink to deep fuchsia, lavender, and even white. But the variation gets even better. Choose bark that is silvery gray, light cream, near white, or, my favorites, light, dark, or medium cinnamon.

These bark colors are what make crepe myrtles so splendid all winter, a quality no other flowering tree can claim. If you are going to mangle the branches, however, your crepe myrtle is going to be deformed, no matter what the bark color.

The common crepe myrtle is prone to powdery mildew and some other unpleasant blights. New varieties are less plagued, and you should do some research before buying, especially regarding mildew resistance.

I have heard about crepe myrtle aphids but have never seen them on my trees. Fortunately these critters have several natural predators, including ladybird beetles and their larvae, parasitic wasps, green lacewings, and an insect-feeding fungus. Let them have at it, and leave the spray for more serious problems.

After pleading with crepe myrtle growers to put down their loppers and chainsaws, I must admit I do clip off flowers when they fade and guess what happens. The crepe myrtle reblooms, possibly three times during a summer.

I also cut off seedpods on branches that are weighed down, and I remove straggly or crossing branches to keep my trees open and outreaching. I also trim off sprouts that emerge at the base of the trees.

It is okay to shape up a plant. It is our duty to do so as gardeners. But, to my mind, it is a sin to distort both the truth and a tree.

Crepe or Crape? I'll Take Both

Weed War

Often people visit my garden and I am always interested in (and a little nervous about) their responses. Just recently a visitor walked around my garden, which, if I do say so myself, was looking especially lush and verdant. We were almost at the end of the tour when she spoke her first words: "You don't have any weeds."

I was astonished. Looking at a summer garden and noticing the absence of weeds but nothing else was shocking. To me, it was like looking at the *Mona Lisa* and commenting on the absence of warts. Not that I compare my garden to a great work of art, though at times it stirs my heart as much as any masterpiece.

It is true that most of my garden has only an occasional weed easily plucked from humus-rich soil during my daily walk around the garden. I mulch my entire garden with shredded leaves or hay in late spring and again in the fall. Years of doing this have changed my sand to sandy loam filled with earthworms, humus, and nutrients.

I am astounded when people tell me how hard and long they work in their gardens and how laborious their garden tasks are. I am convinced that they are doing one of three things: lying, suffering from severe masochism, or trying too hard. As for me, I usually tell the truth, always avoid pain, and follow the adage, "If it's not fun, quit."

My weed-free, pain-free, pleasurable garden is actually a collection of borders and islands and beds. Each started as centipede grass, covered with newspaper (eight sheets thick), then compost, then mulch. When I want to add to an existing border or start a new one, I follow the same process. For the past twenty years, I have never tilled nor dug nor hoed.

After being covered for a season or two, the soil beneath the newspaper-compost-mulch sandwich has become soft, friable, and ready to plant. The centipede and, for the most part, the newspaper layers have become incorporated in the soil where earthworms and microorganisms amuse themselves.

I then plant, sometimes having to dig through soggy newspaper remnants. The roots settle into their new home, tucked under a soft humusy blanket. The newspaper has deprived the sod of sunlight, so the grass dies. The compost enriches the soil. The mulch keeps the soil moist and the soil temperature even.

Another portion of my garden is in the process of becoming a woodland retreat where I plan to sit and ponder and watch frolicking critters at some future date. Right now it is a mass of wiregrass, brambles, and a variety of equally unloved plants. My first step was to make a meandering path through the space. I covered the pathway with overlapping newspaper and covered that with shredded leaves.

I have planted trees, shrubs, herbs, and wildflowers to attract wildlife. I have not tilled or dug up any of this garden except the holes for individual plants. I do not enrich the soil when I plant, and I do not intend to fertilize.

After I plant, I put down newspapers and I mulch with hay (which contrasts distinctly with the pathway of shredded leaves). I pull or dig up large, tough weeds such as brambles since they would meander around and emerge where I had not adequately mulched. I wait until the ground is moist, position myself on a kneeler, and clean out what needs to go. Then I move the kneeler and clean out the next area.

Since this is a wildlife garden, I leave enough weeds along the outside edge or in hidden areas of the garden to provide nectar, shelter, and larval food that may sustain some critters I do not know about.

I have three recommendations for dealing with weeds. The first is to smother the offense, which is what I have described in the newspaper-compost-mulch strategy. You can leave out the compost (as I have done in my wildlife garden), but you need plenty of newspaper layers and a thick mulch of shredded leaves, hay, or pinestraw.

The second recommendation is to inspect your garden almost every day. Depending upon its size, this could take a couple of minutes or, if you dawdle as I do, ten minutes. Just stroll along and, when you see a weed popping through your mulch, bend over and pluck it out and toss it behind the hedge or elsewhere.

Do not bother bundling up weeds and carrying them off in a tarp or wheelbarrow unless you have some use for them. Think of them as a bit of additional mulch and save your energy for something fun.

The third recommendation is what I call the Hugo approach. After Hurricane Hugo, I worked myself into a dither cleaning up and, at the end of the first day, I could not see one bit of difference. My husband, who is very organized and methodical and sometimes bossy, insisted we work one area at a time and get it in good shape before moving on to the next area. My morale improved and eventually the yard was cleaned up.

This is what I do now when I have a mass of Florida betony or briars to contend with. Florida betony (also known as rattlesnake weed) is not a bad-looking plant, but it grows exuberantly from segmented white tubers that do not stop. It would take over the world if left alone, like mini-kudzu.

Again, I prefer to work in moist soil. I move my kneeler about, clean up a designated area, and then move to the next patch. I assign myself so many yards or patches per day and, when I have all the Florida betony cleaned out and in the burning barrel, I am a smug but otherwise virtuous woman.

Notice I have not mentioned herbicides. The water table has enough problems without my adding poison to it. My advice is to keep weeding to a minimum. But when it cannot be avoided, think of it as contemplative exercise during which you accomplish something tangible. And you will not have to do it again until next time.

Something that Bugs Me

When I turned on our local NPR station, I caught a glib and well-informed county agent hosting the noonday gardening show. After the usual turf questions, a woman called in to complain frantically about insects that were "all over" her plants. Without any idea of what these bugs were, her husband had sprayed and dusted those critters with two kinds of sevin to no avail.

"Earwigs," said the agent, who did a fine job assuring her that they were harmless.

The woman was quiet during his extended and reasonable response, but, as soon as he was through, she asked, "How do I kill them?" Makes one wonder about the educational value of public radio.

I laughed because the exchange was so absurd. I had a vision of the woman (who I hope is reading this book) and her husband battling an "enemy" they could not identify, and then, after being told the accused was not an enemy at all, continuing to wage war.

Earwigs are certainly not cute but they are harmless and, like 98 or 99 percent of the insect population on this earth, are actually beneficial. In a healthy garden with humusy soil and a diverse insect population, earwigs turn up their noses at green plants and consume aphids, mealybugs, mites, nematodes, and decaying matter. And, best of all, they eat slug eggs.

We tend to think of beneficial insects as those that devour our garden's evildoers.

Actually, insects are beneficial in even more important ways. With their very lives, insects provide sustenance for birds we enjoy seeing in our gardens and in the natural environment. Talk about self-sacrifice. They also feed frogs, toads, turtles, and other creatures that knowledgeable gardeners invite to the feast.

What would our gardens be without insects? They would be a mass of mammalian waste, especially if we have pets. And they would be a graveyard of birds, rodents, insects, and other animal life that die in our yards. It happens. Everything dies somewhere. Insects feed on decomposing plant and animal material and hasten the decomposition process.

Even the most fastidious gardeners have learned to love compost and will discuss it at the drop of a sun visor. The fact is that, contrary to the bumper sticker slogan, compost does not just happen. It develops because insects and microorganisms make it their life work to turn garbage into dirt. God bless them all.

Through pollination, insects provide one in every three mouthfuls you swallow, that is, if you are eating your fruits and vegetables. We tend to think of honey bees as the great pollinators but plants are actually pollinated by a variety of bees, wasps, ants, butterflies, moths, flies, and beetles, as well as birds and bats.

Think of it this way: The world would continue (and in some ways improve) without human beings but would literally die without insects. We are indebted to them for providing food for other creatures, for doing away with waste products and animal corpses, and for ensuring ample plant life to feed the multitudes.

Am I going to let insects devour my favorite plants? Am I going to let my lawn turn into one big fire ant hill? Hardly. But the first step in insect control is to identify the enemy and then weigh the alternatives. Who is eating my leaves? How important is the plant? What are my alternatives to adding poison to an already polluted earth? What is the least-damaging solution to my problem?

For fire ants, I broadcast a bait that is harmless to mammals and birds over my yard in spring and early fall. Since fire ants were an accidental import and not a native insect who contributes to our ecosystem, it seems okay to, if not eradicate them, at least limit their population explosion.

I use a corn starch–based product for slugs when serious damage becomes apparent. (Where are those earwigs when you need them?) This is a specific pesticide that affects only slugs and not insects or other creatures such as rabbits, frogs, small children, Labrador retrievers, or schnauzers.

Other than fire ants and slugs, I let nature take its course. I stopped using any other pesticides, including organics, years ago. I went cold turkey and never looked back. When I see a few harmful insects, I am confident that help is on its way.

My garden is rich in beneficial insects that have been lured by the absence of pesticides and the presence of a garden as diverse as I can make it. A vital part of that diversity is plants that attract beneficials and a population of insects to keep the beneficials well-fed and content.

If a plant succumbs to insect damage or disease, I just remove it and plop it in the burning barrel, but I cannot remember the last time I had to do this.

Electric zappers damage your electricity bill more than the insects in your yard. In fact, zappers lure beneficials while eradicating very few mosquitoes.

Attract dragonflies to your yard instead. A common name for dragonflies is "mosquito hawks" and for good reason: They regularly consume 100 mosquitoes and larvae every thirty minutes. If you have a fishpond, you probably have dragonflies. You can also put up three-foot-high poles (bamboo is the wood of choice) in sunny spots in your yard, and they will come.

For lacewings, plant yarrow, dill, white cosmos, and fennel. For ladybugs, plant Queen Anne's lace, coriander, tansy, small marigolds, zinnias, caraway, spearmint, and buckwheat.

You can even mix up your own bug food: one part whey or brewer's yeast, one part sugar, and up to ten parts water to spray or spread. I have not tried this myself and, if you decide to do so, I suggest you not mention it at the next party you attend. We gardeners raise enough eyebrows talking compost.

CHAPTER 6

Winnowing

Garden writers and gardeners alike pass along
what we learn and what we love, little enough
to give in return for what we are given.

Walking in a Woodland of One's Own

Somewhat smugly, I describe myself as an unmaterialistic person. The older I get, the less I need to possess. Of course, the world is full of objects I admire in other people's houses or in shops and museums. I just do not need to own them, especially since they need dusting to look their best. If someone else owns them, he or she does the dusting and I enjoy the looking.

However, I confess that there is something I covet and it has to do with gardening. Or not gardening, depending upon how you look at it.

I want a woodland of my own. I want my woodland to be dappled with shade but open to light. I want it to look as if nature designed it as a showcase for berries and nuts and seedpods, and as a sanctuary for small creatures who go about their business of surviving, reproducing, and recycling.

I want a winding path through my woodland I can stroll along without disturbing spiderwebs and other habitats. I want places to sit so I can watch or think or dream. And I want something to wonder about everywhere I look.

I would include a couple of bird feeders, a birdbath, puddles of muddy water for butterflies and toads and lizards. Native shrubs would edge the path and create secret places. Of course I want ferns and flowering plants and vines that wander on the ground and up the trees.

I want piles of brush and groundcovers for hiding places. I want some stumps and dead branches to harbor insects and invite birds that eat them.

As I sit here at my word processor, I see my woodland clearly. It is a respite for me, a playground for grandchildren, and a place where things happen as nature intends. Life begins, thrives, and ends.

In the past few months, I have visited some woodlands that made me realize how much I wanted one of my own. Two are open to the public: a walk up a wooded hillside between a zoo and a botanical garden, and a boardwalk through a swamp filled with giant cypresses.

Both are visually breathtaking. Neither walk requires hiking skills or gear, but the heart beats faster with pride and gratitude because we live in a country that supports such treasures.

Closer to home and to the realm of possibility are three privately owned woodlands and these are the ones I covet. Two are within city limits and the other is in a rural neighborhood. They have made me aware of just how much I desire a woodland of my own and how feasible it is for me to create one.

One of the woodlands is a twentieth or less of a large landscaped estate. This natural area runs along one long side of the property next to a busy street. After cleaning out the wooded area where once there was an access drive and a trailer left to rust, the previous owner closed off the drive, created a meandering pathway, and pretty much left nature to her own devices.

The present owners have no intention of changing this woodland other than adding a few additional native shrubs, a water feature, and a place to sit. They intend to thicken the hedgerow next to the street to furnish more cover and food for birds and privacy for themselves.

The second woodland, also in town, is the result of an astute purchase by the homeowners. Years ago the lot in back of theirs was put on the market and they had the foresight to buy it for no other purpose than to leave it alone. It has served as a play area for children and grandchildren and is now a background for their garden.

Along the front border of the woodland is a remnant of an old wooden fence, a poignant reminder of the passage of time and gardeners. Fallen trees and snags have been left as sanctuaries and food sources for insects and birds. Leaves are left to compost. How much more attractive and interesting this woodland is than the acre of grass it might have become.

I am stirred by the contrast between the homeowners' carefully tended garden and this natural backdrop, and I appreciate these gardeners who have the wisdom and sensitivity to leave a large section of property to nature's whims.

The third woodland is the one that really got me yearning. This property is out in the country and has a lovely small garden at the side of the house dedicated to selected plants the gardener is determined to grow and the deer are determined to eat.

She has enclosed this garden with attractive wood fencing and deer-defying mesh. The mixed border of shrubs, grasses, perennials, and herbs surrounds an island of pristine grass. This area and a patch in front of the house take seven minutes to mow. This is a wise gardener indeed who knows what is important and worth doing.

In back of the house is a path bordered with tea olives, viburnums, winter honeysuckle, ferns, and winged bark elm trees. As the path descends through piney woods to a streambed, the plant life becomes a rich assortment of creeping cedar, wintergreen, partridgeberry, lady slippers, and other natives that spring to life without human assistance.

As for my own woodland, at present it can be seen only by me. To other eyes, it is a mess. It is a corner of my suburban lot I am "letting go," planting trees and native shrubs and hoping to achieve the look I know is best designed by nature. A meandering path comes next and, finally, a rustic arbor that invites me to pause and cast all covetous thoughts behind.

Good Friends, Garden Differences

Recently I was showing a friend around my garden, which I thought looked terrific except for a few bare spots where plants had not yet grown into their own. I apologetically pointed out what would be thriving in those bare spots if she came back in a month or two.

The stems of blue salvia flopped around, winding their way through the pink gaura, gray-green artemisia, and whatever else got in their way. Dwarf coreopsis bloomed perkily along the edges in the sunny section and lady's mantle, while not yet in bloom, was on the brink. Yellow woods poppies glowed in deep shade.

My favorite columbines, tall and graceful, were scattered here and there in at least six different rich pastels as well as white. Even the peonies were showing off for the first time in four years. Pink phlox dominated a section of dappled shade, popping up everywhere, though I pull most of it up every year after it blooms.

My garden looked the way I like it to look, at the point when you cannot tell where one plant ends and another begins, as if the whole border were one lush bouquet. And it was still just May.

This large mixed border, over eight feet deep and about one hundred feet long, runs across the back of the yard, backed by a hedge of ligustrum. Even the hedge was in full bloom as my friend and I strolled.

This border swoops around an oval of green grass with a shady island on the side toward the house. My objective for this border is a semi-enclosed "garden room" where I can sit and sip with friends or be alone to read or count my blessings, a place I can share or hide in, depending upon my mood.

My friend, I have to say, was not nearly as enthusiastic as I. She was conspicuously quiet and, though she thanked me nicely for plants I had dug up for her, she never indicated that she was blown away by the vision she was beholding. She never said, "I want my garden to look just this way," or, "How in the world did you accomplish this masterpiece?"

After she left, I went out to my garden to take another look. I felt as if I had just introduced her to my children and she had failed to comment on their good looks, excellent manners, and intelligent remarks. I was not exactly insulted, but I sure was deflated by the absence of oohs and aahs I think my garden deserves.

Then I thought about my friend's garden and realized that, to her, mine probably looked overgrown and messy. Her plants have definitive places and stay where they are assigned. No rampant groundcover such as creeping raspberry or runaway robin winds its way under shrubs, peeks through lamb's ears, or works its way through the perennials and out into the lawn.

My friend shuns invasive plants such as bog sage and artemisias and even stokesia. As a result, her garden is much neater than mine and possesses a sense of order that mine lacks. But I say, "Each to her own." I find rigidity and neatness stifling myself, but the beauty of a garden is in the eye of the gardener.

The morning after my friend visited my garden, I trotted out with clippers to do a little taming. I cut back some of the plants that had indeed become overgrown. I moved a few to less crowded spaces. As a result, I discovered small sideshoots ready to be detached from their mothers and either put them somewhere else in the garden or potted them up for friends and a plant sale.

As I worked my way around the border, which certainly benefited from artful clipping and deadheading, I was reminded that a garden is such a personal expression. If a dozen of us were given the same plants and equal spaces in which to garden, we each would come up with a different design that would become increasingly unique over time.

My friend had made me look at my garden critically, which is always beneficial for creative endeavors. While I was not about to change my garden to please someone else, no matter how dear a friend she is, I looked at my "bouquet" through someone else's eyes and discovered flaws I might not have seen otherwise.

I did some tidying up and breathed with pleasure the aroma of chocolate mint as I pulled it up by the roots. My friend would never have allowed chocolate mint in her garden. No plant grows more enthusiastically. But it smells heavenly, like peppermint candy without the calories.

My friend would never grow wandering groundcovers like lamium with its subtle variegation or chameleon plant that glows with color in sun or shade. She laughed out loud at my creeping raspberry, which I admit does creep, but its crinkly texture and the reddish cast of its leathery foliage make it an asset.

Oregano is out of the question in my friend's border. While I use it as a front-of-the-border edge, she confines hers to a pot. I am not sure mint is allowed on her premises. I cannot blame her for her tidiness in the garden, anymore than I blame her for the neatness of her closets or her dust-free house.

I am delighted that my visitor and I are friends, in spite of our differences, and that we are both gardeners, each creating an Eden of her own design. Is it not, after all, the differences that keep life interesting and the gardens our own?

Good Friends, Garden Differences

Laurie's Garden: A Work in Progress

When I visited the garden of my friend, Laurie, who at 25 is young enough not to lose heart while overhauling the yard of an old house, I was pleased to see that she is doing it just right. Her garden is a rich combination of textures and shapes. She is thinking in terms of sunlight and potential use of space, and selecting plants that call her name.

In other words, she is not following someone else's rules and she is not trying to recreate the original landscape. She retains large shrubs that thrive and extracts plants that either do not appeal to her or have lost their vigor. She hates to cut down old trees but knows there comes a time when this is necessary.

When she found scale on her pittosporum, she did not head for the nearest poison and start spraying without thought to what enemy she was fighting and what effects the "remedy" would have on the environment. (A dormant oil was her ultimate weapon of choice.)

Before Laurie started her garden renovation, a friend presented her with a design to get her started. If you know it is there, that original design is evident, but Laurie has had the wisdom and creativity to make her garden her own by adding and moving plants, and not adhering inflexibly to someone else's vision.

As we strolled, Laurie asked for suggestions about plants that would work well in specific places. When she asked for possible replacements for variegated privet, I suggested *Lespedeza* 'White Fountain,' which is not overused, blooms late in the summer, has gray-green foliage, and turns bright yellow for a few weeks in the fall.

For me, it is the fall display that earns lespedeza's keep. This shrub is deciduous and some people do not like naked stems in their foundation plantings. I like bare branches myself. Plants that lose their leaves in winter are solid and sculptural and, when they leaf out in spring, add an element of rebirth.

If my friend chooses to, she could cut her lespedeza down to the ground in late fall as soon as it loses its leaves. I leave mine for winter interest and cut it down in spring. Lespedeza needs an annual shearing, but does not seem to care when it is done.

Where Laurie wanted a tall plant at the corner of the house behind a large rosemary, I enthusiastically recommended *Fothergilla major* 'Mt. Airy,' which will grow to about six feet. Fothergilla has cream-colored bottlebrush blooms early in the spring, is green and uneventful all summer, but in fall turns startling shades of red: scarlet, bronze, bright orange, and fuchsia. So much more interesting than a plant that is green all year.

Lespedeza and fothergilla would accomplish two things for Laurie's garden (besides attractively filling up space): They will bloom when not many other plants are blooming and they will add spectacular fall color.

Of course, though she is doing her garden just right, I could not help but offer my own preferences, even when not asked (a fault I will probably not conquer in this lifetime).

Laurie's garden is too green. She has little gray in her garden and no red at all. I voiced the opinion that she needs to add both as soon as possible.

My own garden is full of grays and gray-greens because I grow herbs such as lamb's ears, lavender, rue, rosemary, curry plant, artemisias, and santolina. The deciduous shrubs, lespedeza, buddleia, and caryopteris, as well as evergreens such as blue-green junipers and cedars, add significant strokes of gray that make greens more vibrant.

Painters have known for centuries what wonders red does for green on canvas or paper. It does the same in the natural landscape. Red foliage and bark add punch, pizzazz, oomph to the greens of a garden and should be present year round.

The red bark of certain crepe myrtles, Japanese maples, and red twig dogwood has star quality, especially in winter when plants are leafless and spare. Burgundy-leafed loropetalums can be trimmed up as trees or left to grow in their natural shrub shapes. True trees with red foliage are purple-leafed plums, smoke trees, and the eastern redbud, *Cercis canadensis* 'Forest Pansy.'

My friend's garden cries out for burgundy barberries that, like loropetalums, are available in varied sizes from the dwarf 'Crimson Pigmy' to the five-foot-tall 'Rose Glow.'

The foliage stars of my garden last summer were a burgundy-leafed hibiscus that grew five or six feet tall, alternathera, perilla, coleus, and castor bean plants trimmed as trees. My garden glowed.

We need more red in our winter gardens as well, and barberries fill the bill until they lose their foliage for a short winter rest. In the fall, heat up your garden with *Itea virginica* 'Henry Garnet.' If you are really serious about red, plant *Enkianthus* 'Red Bells,' which is seen not nearly enough, at least by me.

Euonymus alatus (burning bush) provides spectacular color in fall, but buyer beware. This is when botanical lingo proves its value. There are euonymuses and then there are euonymuses, and not all of them burn scarlet. In fact, even *E. alatus* has degrees of redness so if you want real fire, look for cultivars such as 'October Glory,' 'Nordine,' or 'Rudy Haag.'

Laurie's garden will always be a work in progress. She will never sit back and say, "That's all. I've got it just the way I want it." Fifty years from now, she will be rearranging, asking questions, discovering new plants, pulling out mistakes, and finding things out about herself. And that is what gardening is really about.

204

Other People's Gardens

Through sheer good luck, I have found myself doing considerable wandering around other people's gardens recently. By invitation, of course. I love other people's gardens and visit them with enthusiasm. One of the charms of gardening is that there is always something to learn and someone to share what she or he knows.

A good friend of mine has a garden that goes uphill from the house to the back fence line, an insurmountable burden to most gardeners, but this woman has risen to the challenge by terracing and creating separate small gardens in the center and a mixed border around the perimeter.

Her garden, like mine, is more plant collection than garden. Even in late fall, it was a thing of beauty and order. While we were touring, my friend clutched a black notebook to her bosom. When I finally asked about it, she admitted with a blush that this particular book was a documented description of the entire garden. She has a total of twelve notebooks, most of them topical, one for shrubs, one for perennials, another for wildflowers. You get the idea.

Did I mention that in her former life my friend was a biology teacher? Now her garden is her laboratory and she finds her joy in growing iffy plants with enviable success and in documenting their growth habits and other data. She has a unique collection of wildflowers, unusual shrubs and perennials, and several specimens from the Jefferson garden at Monticello.

Some of the gleanings I gained while touring my friend's garden are that gardeners with quite different work habits can be the best of friends; an uphill battle can be won with honor; and plants respond vigorously to amendments such as alfalfa pellets, chicken manure, and cottonseed meal.

Two more things I learned are that a year-round vegetable garden is possible and need not take up much space at all; and no one should ever say, at least to gardeners like her, "That won't grow here."

Another garden I visited recently is a work in progress, a three-acre estate that had been horticulturally neglected for fifty years. Located in a historic Southern city, it has an awe-inspiring collection of old trees and a natural-growth perimeter providing enclosure and privacy.

The couple who owns the property wisely envisions it as a series of separate gardens: his vegetable garden, their rose garden, her Japanese garden, and so on. This is especially beneficial since they have disparate opinions about how a garden should look.

The front of the property is a classic arrangement with a long entrance drive ending in a circle around a grassy area. They chose to make this entrance garden and the foundation planting formal and had already installed most of the trees and shrubs as well as an irrigation system.

We walked all over the property, envisioning how each of the separate gardens would look. I have to tell you, I was green with envy over the potential but I was also overwhelmed by the work ahead. The couple is doing the gardening themselves and both have busy lives. I sensed frustration and the specter of discouragement.

I made a few recommendations regarding plant placement: underplanting the rose garden with a variety of low-growing herbs such as catmint, calamint, and artemisia; mulching the vegetable garden during the winter to suppress weeds; and so on.

But it was when we went inside the house that I realized what they should do without delay, announcing, as is my habit, "If this were my garden . . ." These folks have a kitchen-sitting room, magnificent in both size and comforts, complete with fireplace and lots of glass windows and doors.

This is where they live, and who wouldn't? One side overlooks the future Japanese garden. The other looks out (through French doors) on a large open expanse, ending with a wooded area, the vegetable garden, and a picturesque old barn.

"This is where you need to start," I said with outward calm, though I wanted to tear outdoors to stake boundaries and then indoors to fax a plant order. I advised them to build a three- to four-foot wooden fence around a reasonable area and, in the center, place the millstone they have turned into a water feature.

I suggested they create a meandering path and turn this space into a cottage garden with a couple of flowering trees, shrubs, an array of perennials, and herbs. I envisioned containers, a bench, vines on the fence, and birdfeeders, all of it visible from the desk and couch and kitchen counter.

This is a garden they can "finish" (as if a garden is ever completed) and enjoy while continuing their busy lives and tackling other sections of their plan. This is the space they look at everyday and, therefore, would most enjoy a view.

What I discovered on this garden visit is that two people with different garden visions can live together happily, as long as there is adequate acreage; and that, once the front yard is planted for public viewing, the next logical step is to complete a garden space for personal gratification.

I also realized that sometimes too much space is a greater challenge than too little, and the whole should be divided into workable parts, especially when you have a gardening staff of fewer than eight.

The most important conclusion, however, is that, with choices about gardens and life in general, a person should usually look at the outside from the inside in making decisions.

207

Passalong Some Friendship

PASSALONG MEMORIES

People who walk around my garden with me are often bemused by my references to favorite plants. Columbine is my favorite. But so is butterfly weed. And celadine poppy is another favorite. When I saw campanulas bloom in England, they too became a favorite.

More than one person has advised me that it is impossible to have more than a single favorite. I beg to differ. I have two sons and each is a favorite. I have five favorite grandchildren and two favorite dogs. Some people have multiple talents or multiple births. I am blessed with multiple favorites.

My all-time favorites in the garden are plants given to me by others. Authors Felder Rushing and Steve Bender wrote one of my many favorite books, *Passalong Plants,* giving a name to all those cuttings, divisions, seeds, and bulbs shared by gardeners whose bounty overflows.

In my garden, I have a white butterfly bush given to me years ago by a cherished friend who left this world much too soon. I have rooted at least a hundred cuttings from this buddleia over the years and passed them along to friends all over the country. How fitting it is that perhaps a hundred white butterfly bushes bloom for gardeners my friend never knew but is connected to by their love of nature and life.

In exchange for the butterfly bush, I presented her an anise hyssop and every time I saw her she mentioned the pleasure the plant gave her. I do not doubt that when the original plant dropped seed, as anise hyssops do, she dug up seedlings and passed them along to friends. That is what gardeners do.

Not long ago I was walking in my garden and spotted a winter iris (*Iris unguicularis*) next to the pathway. Since I had divided my single clump last spring, I was not sure I would get blooms this year, but there it was, dressed in a lovely shade of lavender, looking very much like a short Dutch iris, and blooming on a day when the birdbath was full of ice.

This winter iris had been passed along to me after I raved about one presented in full bloom to a Christmas party hostess.

Years after I received my own winter iris, the woman who passed it along to me called and began by saying, "You probably don't remember me . . ." Remember her? Of course I do. Every time I look at one of the iris clumps (which now number six), I think of her fondly.

My garden is full of plants given to me by other gardeners and, as a result, walking and working in my garden is always a stroll down memory lane. I have known few gardeners who do not have a passion for sharing, for passing along their pleasures and knowledge.

After you have gardened awhile, you too will have plants to pass along to gardening friends. You can even be especially angelic and give plants to people you are not fond of at all. Not only will you give the recipients great joy and be an example of generosity and good will; you will also give yourself the satisfaction of sharing plants you cherish and hearing of their progress over the years.

PASSALONG SNOBS

Not long ago I offered a gardening acquaintance a ferny little yarrow, nicely rooted and seeking a sunny home.

"Isn't yarrow invasive?" she asked.

"It does spread," I admitted, "but it blooms for four months and isn't the foliage pretty?"

"But isn't it rampant?" she continued with a furrowing of her brow, as if I were offering her poison sumac.

"I think of yarrow as enthusiastic," I explained, putting the plant back in the cold frame until a wiser gardener came along. Giving my yarrow to this woman would be like offering a puppy to a collector of china dogs.

Nothing in the garden, not even slugs or mosquitoes, irritates me as much as a passalong snob. A passalong plant is a rooted cutting, a shrub right out of the border, even an envelope of seeds that gardeners give to others who are starting a garden or who remember their grandmothers' gardens fondly. My own garden is full of passalongs, and so are most other gardens I enjoy.

Passalong plants are rarely seen in nurseries or garden centers, perhaps because there is no market for them. Generous gardeners supply the demand and then some. Passalongs transplant or seed happily and thrive with minimal care, giving birth to offspring that also get passed along.

I do not understand why people turn up their noses at plants simply because they grow. Isn't that what we want them to do? In fact, plants typically passed along, such as larkspur, cleome, plume poppy, phlox, and obedient plant, are the mainstays of trendy English cottage gardens seen in toney magazine layouts and on garden tours.

I have never found invasive plants a problem since I am in my garden almost every day for at least a quick walk-through. The solution to a plant out of place is simple (and, I might add, healthful). The gardener just bends over, pulls the culprit up, and either tosses it aside for composting or pots it up to pass along.

You can assume that when a person gives you a plant or offers it in a plant swap or sale, it is one of those enthusiastic growers. After all, who is going to give you a hard-to-cultivate, pricey specimen? Not me.

But I am generous to a fault in sharing yarrow, swamp sunflowers, violets, phlox, asters, lamb's ear, lemon balm, apple mint, and others of their ilk. Should you take them? Absolutely. They are all beauties. And, before you know it, you will have your own collection of passalongs to share.

Who's in the Habitat?

A garden certainly makes the gardener think, not only about what plant to put in what location but also about the larger themes of life. Walking around my yard, I am reminded almost daily how dynamic nature is, how abundant and full of potential our earth continues to be no matter how we abuse it.

Resilience is an amazing quality that may very well be life's greatest blessing. As human beings we survive horrors, yet pick up the pieces and go on. Given the chance, lakes and oceans recover from pollution, forests reseed, and air is cleansed.

But we have to make continuous effort to restore what we damage. That is what the Backyard Wildlife Habitat Program is all about: restoring habitat that development has damaged or erased.

My garden is a certified Backyard Wildlife Habitat and has been for a number of years, but it is no longer the same garden I described in my application. I have less grass, more water, more brush piles, more feeders, and definitely more pleasure as I am joined by a variety of welcome creatures.

Whenever I add a plant, I consider its benefits to wildlife. Does it have berries? Is it a nectar provider or host? Do birds enjoy the seeds? Is it shelter for beneficial insects? Or toads? Or lizards? Like these guests, I am especially attracted to native plants that belong in the region where I garden.

In my garden, which is a suburban lot of one acre, I am growing a hedge of ligustrums across the back and part way up each side. I say "am growing" because this is a work in progress, about five feet tall, but the goal is ten feet or more. These shrubs will be left unpruned for the most part; no sharp edges or round balls. I am pretty open-minded when it comes to how people garden, but shrubs sheared into rigid unnatural shapes make my teeth clench.

We used to have a tall, handsome hedge of red tips, but they went the way of most photinias. They became straggly and diseased, and I could not bear watching my husband spray them several times a year to no avail, at least no good avail.

I will let these ligustrums grow to full size to enclose my garden and also to provide plenty of nesting area and cover for the birds. My neighbors have cats, so if I want birds to come to my feeders, it is only right that I give them as much protection as possible.

We have many old hickory trees in our yard, as well as pines, oaks, a black gum, and a sparkleberry, all of which were on the property when we built our house almost forty years ago. To my despair, many of our neighbors have taken to clear cutting, but we are determined to keep all our trees that do not threaten the house or us.

We have planted fruit trees, including a fig tree. I would have a fig tree in my yard even if we did not enjoy standing by it in August, eating our fill. A fig tree has substantial structure as well as leaves with varied shapes and glorious color. And, of course, the birds and bees enjoy the figs as much as we do. So does the dog.

I am especially partial to cedars and have planted two but think I need more. Change is inevitable. In a corner of our yard, where I am creating a wild garden, I have added sassafras, elderberry, serviceberry, possumhaw, sourwood, and a mix of other native shrubs, herbs, grasses, and perennials.

A hickory and an oak have come up on their own and I welcome them as good examples for other natives to take root where they wish. Sometimes I am tempted to pull up an unexpected seedling, but I refrain. After all, in an area dedicated to going wild, plants should get to choose their own locations.

Whenever I hear of a plant that attracts butterflies or hummingbirds, I track it down and into the garden it goes. This past summer I was thrilled to be standing next to a *Salvia guarantica,* which is over four feet tall with royal blue flowers, and feel a hummingbird at my shoulder, sipping away without concern for my presence. This is the kind of magic moment that habitat gardeners treasure.

I am similarly excited to see monarch or swallowtail larvae on milkweed and parsley and fennel. I have taken larvae and foliage from their host plants and raised them in a screen-covered aquarium, keeping them supplied with their preferred diet, watching them form chrysalises, and eventually releasing them near a favorite nectar plant. This is pure joy, especially when a child shares the celebration.

My water supply, two pedestal birdbaths and a ground-level dish, is adequate. I am careful to keep the baths filled because birds need a year-round supply for bathing as well as for drinking. A heater is helpful in the winter, but a dripper keeps the water from freezing, like leaving the faucet on to keep the pipes open. If I had a pond to lure frogs, dragonflies, lizards, and other creatures, I might be an even happier woman.

I have two tray feeders for sunflower seeds and other grains and a tube feeder for thistle seed. Last year, I made my own suet cakes and got rave reviews.

I suggest you create a wildlife habitat in one part of your garden and see what a difference you can make even in a small space. Once you decide to make your garden a backyard habitat to be shared with birds, butterflies, small mammals, reptiles, frogs, and insects, your life will never be the same.

Who's in the Habitat?

Say Goodbye to Garden Guilt

I confess: March overwhelms me. I wake up in the night thinking about all I should be accomplishing in the garden, not to mention in the rest of my life. I bewail the realization that, no matter how hard I work, everything will never be accomplished exactly right.

However, I do my best not to worry about undone chores. After all, I ask myself, what difference does it make if butterfly bushes do not get reduced to seven inches or chrysanthemums are not divided? By July, who will know whether weeds were pulled in early spring? Or daylilies moved to the front of the border? Or overcrowded daffodils dug up and spread out?

This is one more thing to like about gardens: They are so much more accommodating than our houses. Undone housework accumulates and in a few months adds up to disaster. Believe me, I know. But undone garden chores go unnoticed once flowers bloom and foliage flourishes.

Chances are no one will notice your flaws unless you tell . . . which, for some unaccountable reason, most gardeners cannot stop ourselves from doing. We have a compulsion to confess. What is it about us?

"I never got around to cutting back those grasses," you admit to every garden visitor.

"I should have divided the shasta daisies," you lament. "I did not weed the wild garden. . . . Would you believe I never pruned the hydrangeas?" We cannot keep our mouths shut and our consciences clear.

I do not recommend that we ignore garden tasks. But we should stop beating ourselves up about jobs we never get around to finishing . . . or starting. Who cares? Who suffers?

Here is today's garden tip. Adopt it and never look back. *Free yourself of garden guilt. Accomplish tasks that seem important or visible, and forget the rest.*

This year I intend to dig up daffodils the day their blooms begin to fade and immediately move them to other places. I know, I know. We are supposed to let daffodil foliage die back but, if I do that, I will no longer be interested in daffodils and will forget where they are and where I want them to go. I have been assured that moving them right away will not affect their blooms next spring . . . and, even if it does, there is always the spring after that. See? Breaking rules is not as difficult as we have been led to believe.

I adore Japanese anemones and, of course, want more. My horticultural greed is insatiable. March is a good time to take root cuttings, so I will dig up a mother plant or two and cut three- or four-inch slices from the roots. Better yet, I could leave the mother plant in the ground, feel around, and still cut root slices.

Either way, I will pot the cuttings in a flat of commercial potting mix. I will place the roots horizontally in the flat so I do not have to consider polarity, which means which end is the top. If you place root cuttings vertically, be sure you know where leaves should emerge. That is the top.

Other perennials easily propagated from their thick fibrous roots are chrysanthemums, Oriental poppies, butterfly weed, Queen Anne's lace, nicotiana, phlox, geraniums, and bleeding hearts. You could plant a whole garden from root cuttings if you needed to.

I divide daylilies, ferns, grasses, and late-blooming perennials in March so they adjust before summer's dry weather and heat. Some divisions I pot up to share with friends or to plant in the fall, but I always find space to tuck in divisions immediately. I prefer my garden lush and crowded so, by July, dirt, mulch, and occasional weeds are no longer visible. Abundant foliage, like a muumuu, covers many faults.

This is the month to start Irish potatoes, onions, mustard, radishes, and other cold-hardy spring vegetables. I scatter seeds of lettuces and stir-fry greens over potting mix in containers. That way I can keep them watered and move them into shade when the weather gets hot, but right now they bask in sunshine.

Cut back early-blooming shrubs such as forsythia and spirea as they finish flowering. Trim liriope, mondo grass, and aspidistra to two or three inches to make way for fresh foliage. Cut back hydrangeas that bloom on new wood. If you are not sure, leave them alone and record their behavior this summer so you will know how to prune next spring.

As I move around the garden cleaning up, planting, and dividing, I keep the wheelbarrow full of shredded leaves or hay so I can mulch as I go. Before I put the mulch down, I spread compost, organic fertilizer, and lime wherever I think it is needed. I am not scientific or organized about this process. I just do it.

I have never been able to remember where bulbs are planted, especially cyclamen and lycoris. I now carry along a bucket of small white pebbles and strew them over the foliage before it disappears so I will not plant anything on top of them. I do not always remember *what* is under the pebbles, but I know it should not be disturbed.

For me, the most important thing for a gardener to do in March or any other time of the year is to have fun. Stroll around every day to discover surprises. Carry clippers to prune what needs pruning, a small saw to take root cuttings, a trowel to dig up misplaced or overcrowded plants, and a basket or pail to carry sideshoots for potting up or replanting, bulbs that need moving, and seedheads ready to shatter.

Well-armed with these tools, as well as a shovel, a wheelbarrow of mulch, amendments, and a pail of pebbles, you can make your way around the garden tidying up a section at a time. If July arrives and you have not made it around the entire garden . . . well, so be it. The sun will come up, the flowers will bloom, and your garden will be a source of joy instead of frustration. That is the way it is supposed to be.

BIBLIOGRAPHY

Help along the Way

These books continue to guide me as a gardener and a garden writer. I return to them for information and advice, but, most of all, for the pleasure of reading fine garden prose by extraordinary writers.

Bender, Steve and Felder Rushing. 1993. *Passalong Plants*. Chapel Hill: University of North Carolina Press.

Dirr, Michael. 1998. *Manual of Woody Landscape Plants*. Champaign, IL: Stipes Publishing.

DiSabato-Aust, Tracy. 1998. *The Well-Tended Perennial Garden*. Portland, OR: Timber Press.

Druse, Kenneth. 2000. *Making More Plants*. New York: Clarkson Potter.

Hill, Madalene and Gwen Barclay. 1987. *Southern Herb Growing*. Fredericksburg, TX: Shearer Publishing.

Lacy, Allen. 1986. *Farther Afield*. New York: Farrar, Strauss, Giroux.

1992. *Home Ground*. Boston: Houghton Mifflin.

1995. *The Gardener's Eye and other Essays*. New York: Holt.

Lawrence, Elizabeth. 1987. *Gardening for Love*. (Allen Lacy, Ed.) Durham: Duke University Press.

1991. *A Southern Garden*. Chapel Hill: University of North Carolina Press.

Mitchell, Henry. 1981. *The Essential Earthman*. New York: Farrar, Strauss, Giroux.

1992. *One Man's Garden*. Boston: Houghton Mifflin.

1998. *Henry Mitchell on Gardening*. Boston: Houghton Mifflin.

Stout, Ruth. 1955. *How to Have a Green Thumb without an Aching Back*. New York: Exposition Press.

Wilson, James W. 1999. *Bulletproof Flowers for the South*. Lanham, MD: Taylor Publishing.

INDEX

abelia, 9, 98, 113

abundance, 145

acanthus, 54, 157, 177

Acer crataegifolium 'Veitchii,' 85

advice, 32, 81, 124, 195, 205

African blue basil, 176

agaves, 182–84

Agave salmiana, 183

aging, xi, 11–13, 58, 150, 178. *See also* fitness

air pollution, 77–79, 211

akebia, 48, 74–75, 165, 166

Akebia quinata, 74–75

Alchemilla mollis, 199

alfalfa meal, 22, 105, 205

alocasias, 156

alstroemeria, 92–93

alternathera, 204

Andropogon, 56

Anemone xhybrida, 28, 29, 54, 215

angel's trumpet, 95

anise hyssop, 208

anise sage, 140, 179–80, 212

annuals: autumn and, 26–27; beauty of, 107; blooms and, 108; buying, 38; compost and, 39, 108; daffodils and, 41; deadheading, 108, 149; design and, 135; foundation planting and, 83–84;

hardiness of, 107; overview of, 107–8; planting, 108; propagating, 172; resilience of, 135; seed saving and, 62; seed starting and, 107; variety of, 133–35; watering, 108. See also *specific annuals*

ants, 2, 165, 192

aphids, 187, 191

apple mint, 162, 210

Aquilegia canadensis, 25

Aquilegia 'McKana's Giant,' 25–26

Aralia spinosa, 53

artemisia: color and, 203; fragrance of, 175, 177; personality and, 199, 200; replanting, 174; roses and, 206

Artemisia annua, 175, 177

Artemisia lactiflora, 174

Arundo donax 'Variegata,' 55

asarina, 76, 166

Asarina 'Joan Lorraine,' 166

Asclepias tuberosa, 106, 141, 208, 215

Asian jasmine, 48

Asiatic lilies, 122

Aspidistra elatior, 80, 156–57, 168, 215

asters, 106, 210

Athyrium nipponicum pictum 'Ursula's Red,' 157

aucuba, 53, 81, 86, 157

cuttings: chrysanthemum, 30; garden tours and, 17, 18; Japanese anemone, 215; overview of, 170–72; salvia, 181; sedum, 29, 116; sharing, 30, 69, 81, 151, 171, 173, 208–10; tools for, 216; variegated, 86. *See also* propagation

cyclamen, 43–44, 54, 216

Cyclamen coum, 43

Cyclamen hederifolium, 43

Cyclamen persicum, 43

cyclone fence, 46, 47, 48

cypress vine: azaleas and, 140; blooms, 76, 134, 166; butterfly bush and, 139–40; seed saving and, 25, 62

daffodils: annuals and, 41; beauty of, 45; borders and, 141; container gardening and, 168; hyacinths and, 41; pansies and, 27, 41; planting, 42; replanting, 112, 214–15; resilience of, 41; thinning, 40

daisies, 36, 106

damp-off, 92

daphnes, 31, 53, 54, 94–95, 157

Datura, 95

daylilies, 124–26, 141, 215

deadheading: annuals, 108, 149; blooms and, 97, 108, 173; butterfly bushes, 139–40; grasses, ornamental, 57; lilies, 123; perennials, 108, 149; salvias, 181; tools for, 99, 108; *Zinnia angustifolia*, 108. *See also* pruning

dead plants, 62–63, 67, 80, 109

deer, 131–32, 197

design: annuals and, 135; borders and, 139–41; container gardening and, 167, 168, 169; fences and,

206; foundation planting and, 82; herbs and, 141; irises and, 128; Mexican sunflowers and, 134; personality and, 200, 202–4, 206–7; replanting and, 62; roses and, 206; xeriscaping and, 118–19. *See also* location; plant selection

devil's walking stick, 53

digging: as gift, 68; double, 5, 34, 105; laziness and, 6, 34; mulch and, 188, 189; replanting and, 105; tools for, 216; woodland gardening and, 189

dill, 193

Dirr, Michael, 185

DiSabato-Aust, Tracy, 149, 151

discovery: gardening as, xi, 5, 61, 67, 101, 104, 216; joy and, 5, 216; in spring, 5, 101, 115

disease: blossom-end rot, 153; bulb rot, 122; burning plants with, 193; caring for plants with, 104; crepe myrtles and, 187; damp-off, 92; fusarium wilt, 152; grass and, 136; grasses, ornamental, and, 56; leafspot, 47; *Lespedeza thunbergii* and, 147; lilies and, 122; pittisporum and, 202; succulents and, 184; tomatoes and, 152, 153; verticillium wilt, 152; virus disease, 122

dividing: *Artemisia lactiflora*, 174; asters, 106; in autumn, 27, 35, 38, 106; buying and, 115–16; cannas, 156; chrysanthemums, 30, 36, 106; colocasias, 156; compost and, 61–62; coneflowers, 106; coreopsis, 106; daisies, 36; daylilies, 126, 215; ferns, 215; fertilizer for, 61–62; goldenrod, 106; grasses, ornamental, 56–57,

pansies, 27; for perennials, 34; potting up and, 93; repotting and, 104; seed starting and, 93; for shrubs, 58–59; for succulents, 182, 183; for tomatoes, 153, 154; when to apply, 22; woodland gardening and, 189. *See also* soil amendments

Ficus carica, 164, 212

fig trees, 164, 212

fire ants, 2, 192

firecracker vines, 76, 134

fish emulsion, 126, 153

fitness, 11–13, 118. *See also* aging; exercise; walks

five-leaf akebia, 74–75

flats, 26

flies, 192

Florida betony, 190

Florida Nursery and Growers Association, 77

flowering tobacco, 95

foliage: alocasias, 156; aucuba, 157; beauty of, 202; cannas, 155; cast iron plant, 156–57; colocasias, 156; compost and, 66–67; fatsia, 156; fig tree, 164; iris, 128, 129; *Lespedeza thunbergii*, 147; propagation and, 180; pruning and, 150; replanting and, 215; spirea, 147–48, 183; yarrow, 209

forests, 3. *See also* woodland gardening

forget-me-nots, 43

Formosa lily, 122–23

forsythia, 215

Fothergilla major 'Mt. Airy,' 203

foundation planting, 82–84, 86, 163

fountain grass, 56

friends: advice and, 11, 32, 124, 202–4, 205; differences with,

199–201; gardens as, 68; gifts and, 68–69; sharing with, 6, 11, 14, 30, 35, 43, 62, 69, 112, 116, 121, 140, 151, 155–56, 170–71, 173, 208–10, 215

frogs, 191, 213

fungicides, 2, 89, 136. *See also* organic gardening

fusarium wilt, 152

Galanthus nivalis, 41

Galium odoratum, 32, 54

gardenias, 157

gardening: aging and, xi, 11–13, 150, 178; cooking and, 16, 176; as discovery, xi, 5, 61, 67, 101, 104, 216; mistakes and, 16; nature and, 5; personality and, 14–15, 16, 19, 124, 129, 199–207; posterity and, xii; Stout, Ruth on, 16; variety and, 133–35. *See also* organic gardening

Gardening with the Enemy, 130

Garden of Eden, 121

garden plots: autumn and, 23; building, 2–3, 5, 6, 23, 72, 105, 125, 152, 188–89; as gifts, 72; grass and, 6, 72; location for, 15; mulch and, 2–4, 6, 23, 52, 72, 105, 125, 152, 188–89; newspaper and, 2, 23, 72, 105, 125, 152, 188; replanting, 68, 105; soil amendments and, 152. *See also* borders

garden tours, 14, 17–19, 81, 196–97, 199–207. *See also* walks

garlic chives, 177

gaura, 199

Gelsemium sempervirens, 48, 74

geraniums, 215

German Johnson, 152

giant striped reed, 55

gifts, 68–70, 71, 77–78. *See also* sharing

225

globe amaranth, 62, 133–34, 175
globe arborvitae, 168
globe-shaped basil, 176
gloriosa lily, 165
Gloriosa rothschildiana, 165
glory-in-the-snow, 41
golden creeping jennie, 54
golden hops, 76
goldenrod, 37, 106, 141
'Goldflame,' 83, 147
gomphrena, 62, 133–34, 175
Goodwin, Nancy, 18, 43–44
gourds, 48, 166
The Graduate, 182
granite chips, 178
grape hyacinths, 41, 42
grape vines, 165
grass, lawn: borders and, 6; chemicals and, 136; cost of, 136; disease and, 136; garden plots and, 6, 72; groundcovers and, 32, 54; moles and, 130; mulch and, 52, 188; newspaper and, 52, 72, 105, 188; organic gardening and, 137; overview of, 136–38; pests and, 136; trees and, 136; watering, 138; weeds and, 136; xeriscaping and, 119–20
grass, native, 137–38
grass, ornamental: borders and, 55; Christmas and, 175; cutting, 57, 67; dividing, 56–57, 215; foundation planting and, 83–84; groundcovers and, 55; hardiness of, 56; overview of, 55–57; shade and, 56; variegated, 86
gray santolina, 81
greed, 170, 196, 215
greens. *See* lettuce; winter greens
groundcover: beneficials and, 31–32; crepe myrtle as, 32, 186; grass, lawn, and, 32, 54; grass,

ornamental, and, 55; herbs and, 32; location for, 33; mulch and, 31, 32–33; personality and, 201; planting, 32–33; shade and, 54; shrubs and, 32, 200; succulents as, 183; variegated, 87; vines and, 32; weeds and, 31; woodland gardening and, 196
grow-lights, 92
guilt, 214–16

habitat, 211–13. *See also* woodland gardening
Hathaway, Anne, 33
hay-scented fern, 157
health, 11–13, 118. *See also* aging; exercise
hedge clippers, 149
hedges, 46–48, 98
Helianthus angustifolius, 37, 106, 149, 210
hellebores, 54
Helleri holly, 82–83
hens-and-chicks, 182–84
Hera, 121
herbicides, 2, 6, 136, 190. *See also* organic gardening
herbs: beneficials and, 177; design and, 141; drying, 23–24, 176; fertilizer for, 162; fresh, 23–24; groundcovers and, 32; overview of, 176–78; reseeding, 177; roses and, 206; soil and, 178; sun and, 178; watering, 178; in winter, 81. *See also specific herbs*
Hercules, 121
hibiscus, 204
hickory trees, 212
Hill, Madalene, 177–78
"Hints from Heloise," 8
hoeing, 188

Index

holly, 10, 59, 82–83, 98, 99
holly fern, 168
honeysuckle, 75, 198
hops vine, 165, 166
hormones, 172, 173
hostas, 32, 157
houseleeks, 182–84
Houttuynia cordata, 31, 54, 168, 201
Huff, Ruby, 159–60
Hugo approach, 190
hummingbirds: Aurelian lilies and,
    122; butterfly bushes and, 139,
    140; cypress vine and, 76, 139,
    166; exotic love and, 134; herbs
    and, 177; honeysuckle and, 75;
    pineapple sage and, 180; salvia
    and, 134, 140, 179, 180, 181, 212;
    trumpet vine and, 75, 165
Humulus lupulus, 76
hyacinth bean, 76, 166
hyacinths, 41, 42, 76, 166
hydrangea: buying, 110; Christmas
    and, 174; dead, 109; fences and,
    75–76; groundcover and, 31;
    lacecap, 97, 110; overview of,
    109–11; potting up, 173;
    propagation of, 170–71; pruning,
    9–10, 67, 97, 109–11, 215; shade
    and, 53; variegated, 87; vines and,
    75–76, 110
Hydrangea anomala petiolaris,
    75–76, 110
Hydrangea arborescens 'Annabelle,'
    53, 97
Hydrangea macrophylla, 53, 87, 109,
    110
Hydrangea paniculata, 97, 109–10
Hydrangea quercifolia, 97, 109

Ilex cornuta 'Burfordii Nana,' 82–83
Ilex crenata 'Helleri,' 82–83

Imperata cylindrica 'Red Baron,' 55
Indian grass, 56
indigofera, 148
Indigofera amblyantha, 148
insecticides. *See* pesticides
insects: as beneficials, 63, 191–93;
    birds and, 191–92; columbines
    and, 106; compost and, 192; crepe
    myrtles and, 187; food for, 191–92,
    193; grasses, ornamental, and, 56;
    herbs and, 177; leaf-miners, 106;
    organic gardening and, 192–93;
    pesticides and, 192–93; wildlife
    and, 191–92; woodland gardening
    and, 196, 197. See also *specific
    insects*
Iowa State University, 96
Ipomoea batatas, 76, 149–50
Ipomoea purpurea. See cypress vine
Ipomoea quamoclit. See cypress vine
irises, 32, 41, 127–29, 208–9
Iris unguicularis, 208–9
islands, 52–54
Itea virginica 'Henry Garnet,' 53, 204
ivy, 33, 48, 78

Japanese anemone, 28, 29, 54, 215
Japanese blood grass, 55
Japanese iris, 128
Japanese painted fern, 157
jasmine, 48, 74, 165, 168
joe pye weed, 132, 140
jonquils, 41
journals: garden tours and, 17–18;
    generally, 72–73, 205; for
    pruning, 9–10, 97, 110–11; in
    winter, 80. *See also* calendars
junipers, 32, 203

Keil, Eric, 77
kelp meal, 22, 34, 105

Index

pineapple sage, 180

pine trees, 212

pittosporum, 10, 82, 83, 202

planting: annuals, 108; aucuba, 157; in autumn, 27, 36, 38, 42, 56, 58, 62, 121, 172, 185; bulbs, 40–42; camellias, 89; cannas, 157; cast iron plant, 157; chrysanthemums, 30; colocasias, 157; compost and, 108, 122, 125; container gardening and, 168; crocus, 42; *Cyclamen hederifolium*, 43; daffodils, 42; daylilies, 125–26; depth of, 42, 43, 45, 58; in dolomitic lime, 125; fatsias, 157; ferns, 71, 157; grasses, ornamental, 56; groundcovers, 32–33; hedges, 47; hyacinths, 42; Japanese anemone, 28, 29; lilies, 121–22, 123; lycoris, 44, 45; manure and, 125; mulch and, 125, 128, 189; newspaper and, 189; pansies, 27, 38; perennials, 27, 35, 36, 62, 185; propagation and, 172; rootbound plants, 58, 72; *Sedum* 'Autumn Joy,' 29; shrubs, 47, 58–60, 62, 72, 185; soil amendments and, 125, 128; in spring, 29, 56, 62, 121, 123, 172; succulents, 182–83; in summer, 172, 185; swamp sunflowers, 106; time for, 27, 29, 36, 38, 42, 56, 58, 62, 71, 72, 91, 121, 123, 172, 185; tomatoes, 153; tools for, 5; trees, 62, 185; tropical gardens, 157; tulips, 42; violas, 38; watering and, 108, 125; in winter, 71, 72 *See also* seed starting; transplanting

plant selection: autumn and, 16; camellias, 90; for container gardening, 168; crepe myrtles, 186; for foundation planting,

82–84; garden tours and, 19; pests and, 132; seasons and, 15–16; shrubs, 59, 84; spring and, 16; wildlife and, 211; xeriscaping and, 119. *See also* buying; design

plectranthus, 157

plume poppy, 210

plum trees, 203

Pluto, 161

poinsettias, 95

poisonous plants, 94–96, 158

pollination, 192

pollution, 77–79, 211

poppies, 208, 210, 215

possumhaw, 212

posterity, xii

potatoes, 95, 215

pothos, 78

potting mix: container gardening and, 167; potting up and, 26, 61, 71, 93, 116, 215; propagation and, 116–17, 172; repotting and, 103; salvias and, 181; seed starting and, 26; tomatoes and, 154

potting up: *Artemisia lactiflora*, 174; columbines, 26; coreopsis, 173; fertilizer for, 93; hydrangeas, 173; Japanese anemone, 215; offshoots, 61; perennials, 150; potting mix and, 26, 61, 71, 93, 116, 215; propagation and, 117, 172, 215; salvias, 181; size and, 180. *See also* repotting

powdery mildew, 187

Powis Castle artemisia, 81

privet, 46–47, 202

propagation: of agave, 183; of annuals, 172; of bleeding hearts, 215; of butterfly weed, 215; buying for, 115–16; of chrysanthemums, 215; foliage and, 180; of geraniums, 215; of hydrangeas, 170–71; of Japanese anemone, 215; joy and, 117; moisture and, 171; of nicotiana, 215; overview of, 116–17, 170–72; of perennials, 172, 215; of phlox, 215; of poppies, 215; potting up and, 117, 215; of Queen Anne's lace, 215; of salvias, 181; of sempervivums, 183; size and, 180; of succulents, 183, 184; time for, 172; tomatoes and, 174; tools for, 171, 172, 216. *See also* cuttings; dividing

Prosperine, 161

pruning: abelia, 9, 98, 113; amount of, 150; in autumn, 26, 202–3; azaleas, 9, 113; barberry, 98; bearded iris, 127; blooms and, 9–10, 97, 98, 149–51, 186; boxwood, 98; buddleia, 9, 67, 97, 99, 112, 147; butterfly bushes, 9, 139–40; calendars for, 97, 110–11; camellia, 88–89, 89–90; cleaning and, 150; clethra, 98; cleyera, 10, 98; confederate jasmine, 74; coppicing, 98; crepe myrtles, 51, 99, 149, 185–86, 187; daylilies, 126; foliage and, 150; hedges, 98; holly, 10, 98, 99; hydrangeas, 9–10, 67, 97, 109–11, 215; indigofera, 148; journals for, 9–10, 97, 110–11; lacecap, 97; lantana, 9, 97, 147, 160; *Lespedeza thunbergii*, 147, 202–3; ligustrum, 98, 99, 112, 211–12; loropetalums, 49, 50, 51; Mexican bush sage, 180; Mexican orange shrub, 173; Mexican sunflowers, 149; mint, 162; mistakes with, 150; mophead, 97; overview of, 97–99; perennials, 39; pests and, 150; pittosporum,

10; privet, 46–47; root pruning, 23; roses, 75; Rule of Five and, 8; Rule of Green Thumb for, 9–10, 149–51; sasanquas, 98; shearing, 98; shrubs, 9–10, 67, 82, 83, 88–89, 97–98, 211–12, 215; spirea, 9, 98, 215; in spring, 9, 112, 113, 160, 202–3, 215; in summer, 10, 109, 111, 149–51; summersweet, 146; swamp sunflowers, 106, 149; thinning, 9, 40, 98; time for, 9–10, 26, 67, 97–98, 109, 110–11, 112, 113, 149–51, 160, 202–3, 215; tip-pruning, 98; tools for, 5, 99, 149, 150, 216; trees, 149; trumpet vine, 165; variegation and, 87; vines, 149–50, 165; vitex, 98, 149; walks and, 2, 165; in winter, 9–10, 67, 97–98, 109, 110, 111. *See also* deadheading

pulmonaria, 132

purple-leaf sugarcane, 55

Queen Anne's lace, 193, 215

radishes, 215
rain lilies, 44
raised beds, 13
rattlesnake weed, 190
Raver, Anne, 77, 78
redbud trees, 203
red mustard, 168
red tips, 47, 211–12
renovation, 34–35, 41–42, 202–4, 206–7. *See also* cleaning
repotting, 71–72, 103–4, 185. *See also* potting up
reseeding plants, 134, 135, 166, 177, 180
resilience: of annuals, 135; of columbines, 106; of daffodils, 41;

of life, 211; of Mexican sunflowers, 108; of perennials, 105

rhubarb, 95

Ricinus communis, 94, 116, 204

rootbound plants, 58, 72, 103, 153, 185

root pruning, 23

roots: buying and, 103; pruning, 23; rootbound plants, 58, 72, 103, 153, 185; watering and, 6

rosemary, 23, 81, 168, 175, 203

roses, 54, 75, 90, 166, 206

royal fern, 157

Royal Horticultural Society, 130

rubber plants, 78

Rubus calycinoides, 31, 54, 200, 201

Ruby's shrubs, 160

rudbeckia, 36, 37

rue, 54, 81, 141, 203

Ruellia brittoniana, 141

Rule of Five, 8–9, 9–10. *See also* cleaning

Rule of Green Thumb, 9–10, 149–51. *See also* pruning

runaway robin, 200

Rushing, Felder, 208

Saccharum officinarum 'Pele's Smoke,' 55

sage, 23, 179. *See also* salvia

salvia: dividing, 36, 106; favorites, 134, 141; overview of, 179–81; personality and, 199, 200; wildlife and, 134, 140, 212. *See also* sage

Salvia coccinea, 134, 141, 180

Salvia elegans, 180

Salvia farinacea 'Victoria,' 179

Salvia guaranitica, 140, 179–80, 212

Salvia leucantha, 141, 180

Salvia splendens, 180

Salvia superba, 180–81

Salvia uliginosa, 179, 200

Sambucus canadensis, 85–86

santolina, 203

sasanquas, 98

sassafras, 212

scale, 202

schefflera, 78

Schizophragma hydrangeoides, 75–76, 110

scillas, 41

sea lavender statice, 174

seaweed emulsion, 153

sedge, 56, 87

sedum: in autumn, 28, 29; borders and, 141; cuttings, 29, 116; dividing, 36, 106, 116; groundcovers and, 32; overview of, 182–84

Sedum 'Autumn Joy,' 28, 29, 141, 183

Sedum mackinoi 'Ogon,' 183

Sedum 'Neon,' 183

Sedum 'Purple Emperor,' 116, 183

seed saving, 25, 62, 92, 108

seed sharing, 62, 81, 151

seed starting: annuals, 107; in autumn, 25–27, 123; cleome, 107; columbine, 25–26; compost for, 26; fertilizer for, 93; flats for, 26; Formosa lily, 123; joy and, 117; lettuce, 26, 215; potting mix and, 26; seed saving and, 92; in spring, 107; time for, 25–27, 38, 91–93, 107, 123; vermiculite for, 26, 91, 92; watering and, 91; in winter, 38, 91–93, 107; zinnias, 107. *See also* planting

sempervivums, 182–84

sensitive fern, 157

September 11 tragedy, 77–78

serissa, 168

233

serviceberry, 212

shade: camellias and, 89; cast iron plant and, 157; colocasias and, 156; crepe myrtles and, 185; ferns and, 157; grasses, ornamental, and, 56; groundcovers and, 54; irises and, 128; lantana and, 159; *Lespedeza thunbergii* and, 147; lilies and, 123; mint and, 162; overview of, 52–54; salvias and, 181; spirea and, 147; succulents and, 182; summersweet and, 146; xeriscaping and, 119

sharing: advice, 11, 81, 124, 195, 205; cleaning and, 210; cuttings, 30, 69, 81, 151, 171, 173, 208–10; dividing and, 11, 35, 116, 155–56; with friends, 6, 11, 14, 30, 35, 43, 62, 69, 112, 116, 121, 140, 151, 155–56, 170–71, 173, 208–10, 215; generally, 151; joy and, 6, 14; mint, 161; personality and, 14, 124; renovation and, 35; seeds, 62, 81, 151; size and, 180. *See also* gifts

shastas, 106

shearing, 98

shrubs: aging and, 58; beauty and, 59–60; borders and, 59–60; buying, 58, 84; color and, 203; compost for, 58; dogs and, 172; fertilizer for, 58–59; for foundation planting, 82–84, 86; groundcovers and, 32, 200; hedges and, 46–48; mulch and, 58–59; planting, 47, 58–60, 62, 72, 185; plant selection for, 59, 84; pruning, 9–10, 67, 82, 83, 88–89, 97–98, 211–12, 215; replanting, 23; Ruby's shrubs, 160; soil amendments for, 58–59; summer and, 146–48; watering, 59; wildlife and, 211–12; woodland gardening and, 196, 197. *See also* *specific shrubs*

Siberian iris, 32, 128

signs, 69

slugs, 191

small pine, 168

smoke trees, 203

snowdrops, 41

snow peas, 166

soil: bulbs and, 40–41; camellias and, 89; compost and, 188–89; container gardening and, 167; daylilies and, 126; drainage and, 40–41; ferns and, 157; grasses, ornamental, and, 56; herbs and, 178; lantana and, 159; lavender and, 178; laziness and, 152; lilies and, 122; mint and, 162; mulch and, 2–3, 6, 22, 120, 126, 188–89; organic gardening and, 56; perennials and, 34–35; summersweet and, 146; zephyranthes and, 44. *See also* soil amendments

soil amendments: autumn and, 22–23; compost and, 113; container gardening and, 167, 168; *Cyclamen hederifolium* and, 43; daylilies and, 126; garden plots and, 152; generally, 205; as gifts, 68; irises and, 128; organic gardening and, 22–23, 28, 34, 41, 58–59, 113; perennials and, 34–35, 105; planting and, 125, 128; replanting and, 68, 105; shrubs and, 58–59; soil tests and, 22–23; tomatoes and, 153, 154; tools for, 216; when to apply, 22–23; woodland gardening and, 189. *See also* fertilizer

soil tests, 22–23, 113
solidago, 36, 37–38
Solidago rugosa 'Fireworks,' 37
Solidago sphacelata 'Golden Fleece,' 37–38, 141
Solidago spp., 37, 106, 141
Sorghastrum, 56
sorrel, 151
sourwood, 212
Southern shield fern, 157
southernwood, 153
sparkleberry trees, 212
Spartina, 56
spearmint, 162, 193
spider lily, 44, 45
spider plant, 78
spirea: blooms and, 147–48; foliage and, 147–48; for foundation planting, 82, 83; pruning, 9, 98, 215
Spirea xbumalda, 82, 83, 147–48
stokes aster, 36, 173, 200
stonecrops. *See* sedum
stooling, 98, 113
Stout, Ruth, 12, 13, 16
Stuyvesant Hight School, 77–78
Stylophorum diphyllum, 54, 199
succulents, 182–84
summersweet, 53, 146
sun: cannas and, 156; colocasias and, 156; ferns and, 157; herbs and, 178; irises and, 128; lantana and, 159; lavender and, 178; laziness and, 152; *Lespedeza thunbergii* and, 147; lilies and, 123; mealycup sage and, 179; mint and, 162; panicle hydrangea and, 109–10; salvias and, 181; spireas and, 147; succulents and, 182, 183; summersweet and, 146; xeriscaping and, 119

sunflowers, 55, 62. *See also* Mexican sunflowers; swamp sunflowers
Swallowtails, 140
swamp sunflowers, 37, 106, 149, 210
sweet annie, 175, 177
sweet autumn clematis, 75
sweet pepperbush, 53, 146
sweet potato vines, 76, 149–50
sweet shrub, 146–47
sweet woodruff, 32, 54
Swiss chard, 168
switch grass, 56, 116

tabouli, 162
Tagetes lemonii, 141
tall indigo, 148
tansy, 177, 193
tea olives, 198
teasel, 175
Thai basil, 116, 141, 176
thinning, 9, 40, 98
Thompson, Janet, 130–31
thyme, 23, 168, 175, 176
tilling, 2, 4, 188, 189
time, xi
tip-pruning, 98
tithonia, 62, 108, 134, 149
toads, 63, 191, 196, 211
tomatoes, 152–54, 174, 177
tools: aging and, 12, 150; for cleaning, 216; for cuttings, 216; for deadheading, 99, 108; for digging, 216; for dividing, 56–57, 116; for mulch, 216; for planting, 5; for propagation, 171, 172, 216; for pruning, 5, 99, 149, 150, 216; for replanting, 9, 216; for soil amendments, 216; for weeds, 189, 190
Trachelospermum jasminoides, 48, 74, 165

235

transplanting: *Artemisia lactiflora*,
174; blooms and, 214–15;
calendars and, 112; container
gardening and, 169; daffodils, 112,
214–15; design and, 62; digging
and, 105; foliage and, 215; irises,
128; Japanese anemone, 28, 29;
lycoris, 45; mulch and, 35, 119;
offshoots, 61; perennials, 35, 105-
6; repetition of, 53, 62; root
pruning and, 23; Rule of Five
and, 9; shrubs, 23; soil
amendments and, 68, 105; in
spring, 112; in summer, 151; time
for, 112, 151; tools for, 9, 216;
trees, 23; watering and, 35, 119;
xeriscaping and, 119

trees: color and, 203; as gifts, 69;
grass and, 136; planting, 62, 185;
pruning, 149; replanting, 23;
variegated, 85–86; wildlife and,
212. See also *specific trees*

tropical gardens, 155–57

trumpet vine, 75, 159, 165

tulips, 41, 42

turtles, 191

urine, 131

variegation, 85–87, 156, 157, 168

variety, 133–35

vegetable gardening, 205, 206, 215.
See also *specific vegetables*

vermiculite, 26, 91, 92

veronica, 9, 36, 106

Veronica peduncularis, 9

verticillium wilt, 152

viburnums, 47, 53, 198

Vinca major, 31, 33

vines: fences and, 46, 47, 48, 74–76,
166; groundcovers and, 32; joy

and, 165, 166; organic gardening
and, 165; overview of, 165–66;
pruning, 149–50, 165; roses and,
166; woodland gardening and,
196

violas, 38

violets, 43, 210

Virginia sweetspire, 53

virus disease, 122

vitex, 98, 149

voles, 131

walks: garden tours and, 19; location
and, 15; pruning and, 2, 165;
weeds and, 188, 189; in winter, 80;
woodland gardening and, 196.
See also *fitness; exercise; garden
tours*

wasps, 192

water gardening, 142–44, 193, 213

watering: annuals, 108; cannas, 156;
cast iron plants, 157; container
gardening and, 167, 168; crepe
myrtles, 185; daylilies, 125–26;
depth of, 6; grass, lawn, 138;
grasses, ornamental, 56; herbs,
178; irises, 128; lantana, 159;
lavender, 178; mealycup sage, 179;
mint, 162; mulch and, 3, 6, 120;
nature and, 2; perennials, 107;
planting and, 108, 125; rain lilies,
44; replanting and, 35, 119; roots
and, 6; salvias, 181; seed starting
and, 91; shrubs, 59; succulents,
183; tomatoes, 153; xeriscaping
and, 118–19, 120, 138

weeds: aging and, 12; cleaning and,
189–90; exercise and, 165; grass
and, 136; groundcovers and, 31;
herbicides and, 190; joy and, 188;
laziness and, 6; mulch and, 3, 4,

236

6, 12, 114, 188–89, 206; newspaper and, 3, 6, 105; organic gardening and, 165, 190; overview of, 188–90; Rule of Five and, 8–9; tools for, 189, 190; walks and, 188, 189; woodland gardening and, 189

weigela, 98, 113

The Well-Tended Perennial Garden, 149

wildlife: borders and, 139–41; gardening with, 130–32; habitat for, 211–13; insects and, 191–92; nature and, 211; plant selection and, 211; shrubs and, 211–12; trees and, 212; water gardening and, 143, 144; woodland gardening and, 189, 196. See also *specific wildlife*

Wild Ones, 137

Wilson, Jim, 153

wintergreen, 198

winter greens, 38, 80–81, 168

Wisley, 130

wisteria, 75, 95

Wisteria frutescens 'Amethyst Falls,' 75

Wolverton, William, 77, 79

woodland gardening, 189, 196–98, 212. *See also* habitat

woods poppies, 54, 199

wormwood, 81

Wustin, Alfred, 14

xeriscaping, 118–20, 138

yarrow, 106, 175, 193, 209, 210

yellow jessamine, 95

yew, 95

yucca, 132

zebra grass, 86

zephyranthes, 44

Zephyranthes candida, 44

Zephyranthes citrina, 44

Zephyranthes grandiflora, 44

zinnia, 25, 62, 107–8, 134, 193

Zinnia angustifolia, 108, 134

zoysia grass, 137

About the Author

By some genetic fluke, Margot Rochester emerged from a city dwelling family as a passionate gardener. Born in Los Angeles and raised in various parts of California and New York, she likes to say she discovered gardening at a bookstore at the University of Michigan. After graduating, marrying, and moving to South Carolina, she started some serious digging in.

While admitting to her share of failures over the course of almost forty years, her enthusiasm never wavered. Gardening is her passion. So is writing about gardens. She has been a freelance garden columnist for fifteen years. *Earthly Delights* is her first book and she is working on her second.

In the midlands of South Carolina and on the Outer Banks of North Carolina, Margot lives with her husband of forty-eight years. Adding zest and joy to their lives are two sons, two daughters-in-law, five grandchildren, and two spoiled dogs.